Israel's Messiah

Israel's Messiah

Restoring Jewish Christology

MICHAEL TUPEK

RESOURCE *Publications* • Eugene, Oregon

Resource Publications
An Imprint of Wipf and Stock Publishers
199 W. 8th Ave., Suite 3
Eugene, OR 97401

www.wipfandstock.com

PAPERBACK ISBN: 978-1-4982-9179-8
HARDCOVER ISBN: 978-1-4982-9181-1
EBOOK ISBN: 978-1-4982-9180-4

04/16/21

Contents

Introduction

THE HEBREW PROPHET ISAIAH said long ago to the nation of Israel, "For to us a child is born, to us a son is given, and the government will be on his shoulders. And he will be called Wonderful Counselor, Mighty God, Everlasting Father, Prince of Peace" (Isa 9:6). This book is a study of the prophesied Messiah given to Israel, who is a Hebrew man in whom the God of Israel had become fully incarnate. This book is also a study that will demonstrate how the Torah of Moses completely described the nature of the God of Israel who is now permanently incarnate in the man Jesus. This book is also an anti-trinitarian study that will refute the Roman Catholic doctrine of the Trinity. The dogma of the Trinity is neither Jewish nor the teaching of the Hebrew prophets, but which is found in the evangelical Christian church as a core belief. The fact of this disconnect creates a serious problem.

This book will argue for the biblical Christology of the prophesied Messiah. A biblical theology means a doctrine that is purely derived from the canon of scripture contained in the Bible without the influence of extra-biblical ideas. This means paying careful attention to only what Moses and the Hebrew prophets have revealed in the Old Testament scriptures, and then paying careful attention to only what Jesus and the Jewish apostles have affirmed in the New Testament scriptures.

The Trinity is usually defined simply as the one true God existing as three eternally distinct divine persons comprised of the Father, the Son, and the Holy Spirit. Somehow each person is the one true God and yet separate from each other. My contention is that the myth of the Roman Catholic Trinity is *not a teaching of the Hebrew prophets* and so would not be a part of the faithful preaching of the apostles of the Messiah Jesus, and therefore not at all derived from the Christian Bible. Rather, the Trinity doctrine arose from a later *misreading* of certain passages of scripture due to the unsanctioned influence of the Hellenistic theologians coming from a pagan and polytheistic Greco-Roman cultural background.

1

The fully developed Trinity doctrine of the triune, or three-person, nature of the Godhead emerged as the dominant doctrine after many years of both theological and political wrangling within the early church, and consequently became the official Imperial theology of the "Christianized" Roman Empire during the fourth and fifth centuries. Now, as then, the teaching is presented as the truest expression of biblical revelation. Now, as then, it is maintained by the dishonest means of mistaken definitions of certain terms, misreadings of certain passages, and circular reasoning. The very first mistake, from a logical standpoint, is the invariable misreading of the prologue to the Fourth Gospel, found in John 1:1–18. In fact, the whole prologue is inexorably misunderstood because the first verse is misread. This passage is really the hinge upon which the whole door of the Trinity doctrine swings. So much is dependent on it that if this passage were not in the Gospel text there would never have been a triune Godhead conceived. Fortunately, once the prologue is read according to the Jewish author's intended meaning, the trinitarian concept will evaporate.

As the Christian community of the early church grew from being a small Palestinian Jewish group to include abundant Gentile converts from the wider Hellenistic environment, there was the momentous mistake made by the Greek theologians by *failing to appreciate the controlling influence of the Hebrew Scriptures* according to its Israelite sense of terminology; that is, the Jewish sense of key terms and concepts which are first encountered during the Israelite culture of the biblical period in the Hebrew Bible, which Christians call the Old Testament. Therefore, Greco-Roman notions naturally filled the void by mis-coloring the Jewish definitions of key terms that they encountered in the scriptural witness to the person and work of the Son of God, Jesus, which are found in the Gospels and apostolic letters of the New Testament.

The Trinity dogma, in its most elementary form, seems to have entered the imagination of the church soon after the apostolic era ended, sometime during the early part of the second century. For examples, Ignatius of Antioch first expresses a regard for a complex Godhead (around 110 AD); and the Letter of Barnabas (written probably around 130 AD) has some language that regards Jesus as the "Son of God" as distinguished from, and not merely as being, the "Son of Man," as though they referred to a purely divine and human nature respectively, and regards him as having an eternal pre-existence before he came into this fallen world, having been present at creation (See Letter of Barnabas 5:5; 6:12; 12:10); and the Letter of 2 Clement also mentions that the Lord Jesus "was first a spirit and then became flesh" (Letter of 2 Clement 9:5).

Amazingly, there is even at this early stage of the church, seen for example in the Letter of Barnabas, the unacceptable senselessness of the author showing *no theological disturbance* about this surprising aspect of God (that he has an eternal son!) even while this letter attempts to review the real purposes of the Old Testament revelation given to Israel! There is no embarrassment nor attempt to defend this aspect. If there is a divine son, should not there be then a divine mother?! There would be no problem providing an explanation if we relied upon pagan mythologies, but it cannot be provided from the completely distinctive Jewish Bible. Nevertheless, no matter how far back we may find this dogma in the uninspired writings of men, if this belief is not plainly taught in the canonical scriptures, then it should be rejected as an error.

The reality is that, instead of defending biblical Jewish monotheism, the Hellenistic theologians who were still obsessed with Greek philosophies forced the biblical testimony through their preferred philosophical meat grinder, which produced the messy myth of the tripersonal God. All the ensuing trinitarian theological developments during the second through fifth centuries were deviations from the inspired scriptures and are to be rejected as rubbish if we wish to be truly biblical in our beliefs.

What the evangelical Christian church is left with is a serious *disconnect* between the religion of Abraham, Isaac, and Jacob and the supposed religion of the apostolic church; a disconnect between the Mosaic religion of Israel and the supposed religion of Jesus and Paul. Most trinitarians would justify this interruption by claiming the Trinity idea is a legitimate abstraction reasoned from the supposed biblical evidence. But once that theological disconnect based upon silence is allowed, then the door is opened to welcome other fanciful doctrines such as the many Catholic errors and the many Jewish myth traditions, and the church will be left never really knowing where to draw the line. These living historical examples are the dangerous results of neglecting the principle of maintaining a *direct connection between clear prophetic disclosure and clear apostolic reflection*. But as I have already suggested, this Trinity dogma, which is a surprise to the new church, should also have been a surprise to the apostolic community. But they know nothing of it.

It should be noted that the Trinity doctrine cannot be historically traced all the way back to the very days of the apostles. Even some of the earliest surviving Christian writings (which did not make it into the biblical canon of scripture), that come from the period just prior to the documented expressions of a belief in a complex Godhead, do not demonstrate any awareness of this notion within their doxologies or discussions. See, for example, 1 Clement (possibly written around 95 AD). However, while it might be informative to review the surviving non-canonical Christian writings, the facts are that they are not inspired, are often fragmentary, and do not provide a clear assessment of the doctrinal beliefs of that period, which was probably varied. Therefore, they cannot be authoritative for our investigation.

What is more important is that we will see that there is simply *no New Testament account of a surprising apostolic announcement of the doctrine of the Trinity with the coming of the Son of God, Jesus.* More than this, there is simply *no disturbance or disputation by the Jewish Christian believers* recounted in the New Testament upon the supposed learning of an *"eternal son of God"* existing alongside the Creator from the eternal past. Furthermore, there is *no account of the non-believing Jewish community taking offense or condemning the surprising teaching of a complex nature of the Godhead* now supposedly revealed by the coming of the Son of God.

When the unbelieving Jewish authorities objected to the messianic claims of Jesus, either during his ministry or during his court-trial before Pilate, they never once presented the charge of polytheism as a ground for executing him and rejecting the claims of the Christian community. This they surely would have, and traditional orthodox Jews object to apparent polytheism to this day. Since its inception from the second century, trinitarianism has remained one of the main hindrances for the traditional Jew to accept the claims of Christianity. Even if we assume that the new revelation was received without objection among the believing Jewish Christian community, still we should find the unbelieving Jews taking offense by it. It is absurd to think that the Jewish leadership would falsify damning testimony against Jesus, as we do read of, but that they would not present perhaps the best reason to indict him.

We do read, in the Fourth Gospel, Jesus being condemned by the Jewish authorities for making himself "equal to God." But this is not the same thing as saying he was condemned for claiming he was a *divine son eternally alongside* the Father, which would no doubt only be construed as Jesus being a second deity alongside God. In the Gospel account, the Jews were offended that Jesus, who appeared to them as a mere man, would dare claim God as his "own Father," which somehow implied divine equality. The rabbis were naturally irritated that a mere man would dare regard himself as divinely related to God. But they were not made aware by anything Jesus had said to them that would indicate he was an *eternal* son of God, which is vastly different. Again, a specific objection to an eternal sonship is not found as a charge against Jesus.

It is my desire to provide a fresh and careful exploration of the inspired scriptures concerning both the subjects of the revealed nature of the

Godhead and Israel's Messiah in order to break the neck of this erroneous Trinity teaching, so that through a better reading of the inspired texts it will eventually bleed out and be jettisoned from the church. This exploration will consider only the Bible and will not regard the ideas and concepts found in the uninspired literature of later Judaism, during the period between the biblical testaments. That is, the "apocryphal," "pseudepigraphic," and "apocalyptic" literature of the late Second Temple period has no real bearing on the matter. The simple reason being that when our Lord discussed his person and calling, these writings were never quoted to support them. Neither did the Gospels nor apostles of Jesus ever look to them. Therefore, I care nothing for them. In fact, they have only contributed confusion to the questions.

Another careful examination of the scriptures is necessary because when the Protestant church reformers had eventually repudiated many Roman Catholic errors, they *failed to perceive the trinitarian doctrine to be as suspicious as the other unwarranted accretions.* There were also, during the Reformation crisis, some anti-trinitarian reactions to the Protestant insistence on the Trinity, but they were, to my mind, inadequate or defective attempts. However, the fact that this Catholic error remains in the church does not prove that it is biblically sound, just as many other mistakes went shamefully unquestioned for so long.

I would probably disassociate myself, as a non-trinitarian, from all of these previous non-trinitarian responses, both ancient and modern, as being not quite theologically sound, or even seriously unsound, and therefore not adequately representing biblical Hebraic monotheism. Biblical monotheism would be more accurately described as Hebraic unitarianism—though I despise the term "unitarian" for its unbiblical historical connotations! If I am considered unitarian, then I am Jewish unitarian, just as Moses and the Jews were unitarian. Here I would also say that the term "monotheism," according to its original meaning, is usually employed as a misnomer since it properly means "only God, none beside him" which falls short of describing the *nature* of the Godhead *inhering* in that supposed only God. The trinitarians will readily insist that they are monotheists. The terms "unitarian" or "trinitarian" more properly refer to the only God's *inner makeup*. Trinitarians assert that they believe in monotheism as well as the Jews, but Israel more accurately held to a God who was one pure personal spirit, who is neither complex nor *divisible* in any sense—unitary in makeup.

One of the most important parts of this examination, from a certain perspective, is the consideration of what the Torah and the writing prophets have disclosed concerning the plan of redemption for mankind's salvation, which certainly involves a human being, and what was disclosed of the Messiah in particular. This is the sure approach that was related in the Fourth Gospel, when Jesus said to the antagonistic Jews, "If you believed Moses, you would believe me, for he wrote about me" (John 5:46); and again, because the entire Jewish Scriptures testify about him (John 5:39). Then having examined Moses and the Hebrew prophets, we must discipline ourselves to carefully review the New Testament perceptions and teachings of the apostles of the Messiah in order to correctly understand what they teach about Jesus, his nature, and his work. If we would be responsible interpreters of the Bible's revelation of the Messiah, we must come to rightly understand the prophets' statements in their Israelite culture, and then we must pay careful attention to what the apostles in turn understood from the prophets.

It can hardly be overstated that, first, we review the prophets' pronouncements, *then* we review the apostles' reflections. We cannot reverse this order! This is the biblical method, as well as the natural progressive unfolding, as evidenced by Paul who protested to King Agrippa that his preaching was "saying nothing beyond what the prophets and Moses said would happen" (Acts 26:22; see Rom 1:1–4; 1 Pet 1:10–12). The correct appreciation of this Hebraic revelation of redemption—unaffected by preconceived church notions—will *ensure the sound preparedness* for interpreting the New Testament disclosure of the nature of this predestined Messiah of redemption.

It is my strong desire to *recover a pure Hebraic Christology* that is honestly consistent with, and worthy of, the foundational Hebrew Bible. That is, a Christology which teaches that the one unitary God of Israel became incarnate by his fully joining himself with the man Jesus of Nazareth; and that this man, in whom now resides all the fullness of the Godhead bodily, is only then the uniquely-begotten Son of God. But for scriptural purity, we must avoid all Greco-Roman influence, which had colored the victorious Imperial theology that was soon ratified since the Roman Emperor Constantine had adopted Christianity as the state religion in the fourth century. I also feel that the Jews who do accept Jesus as the prophesied Messiah should be the very ones who should zealously welcome my convictions since they are ordinarily raised in a true Hebraic unitarian culture, and they should be the most disturbed by the standard Christian teaching on this subject.

It might be claimed by some that I am merely resuscitating the old proto-orthodox doctrine of Modalism, which had become rather dominant when the early church leader Tertullian, in reacting to this doctrine, attempted to safeguard the deity of Jesus by promoting a *new* idea: the essential trinitarian component of the *eternal pre-existence* of Jesus as "God the Son," and that it was he that became incarnate rather than God the

Father. Tertullian was both pugnacious and sarcastic. He employed the label "patripassionism" sarcastically, ridiculing the idea that the Father had "suffered" the crucifixion in the person of the human son. However, he seems stupid also because he was then implying that, in trinitarian understanding, the second member of the Godhead *was* capable of suffering while the first member was not! How then was the pre-existent Son divine? How was the Son's deity different from the Father's? Tertullian's solution preaches nonsense! God in no sense suffered on the cross in himself. And I reject any complex idea of the Godhead.

This shameless attempt to defend the deity of Jesus with this new teaching hatched by Tertullian comes from misreading the New Testament, and is unnecessary, and creates a new religion because it is not at all found in the Hebrew prophets. It will be demonstrated that there are only two natures that are regarded in the New Testament consistently. These two being the one unitary deity and the one real soul, flesh, and blood of the man Jesus, *in whom God became incarnate*. These two real persons are recognized because they are comprised of the two natures: divine and human. They have a real and unforced distinction between them, as opposed to the supposed distinctions between the imagined three *personae* within the trinitarian Godhead. The Spirit of God is only an extension of the *presence* of this one unitary God. The Spirit does not constitute another distinct person.

Prior to the rise of trinitarianism, there must have been an apostolic belief in a unitary God held in the post-apostolic church, in accordance with the Jewish Scriptures, that was biblically sound. It was of a *reactionary* nature of leaders such as Justin Martyr and Tertullian who spawned the wild and groundless theology of a complex Godhead, supposing to defend the deity of Jesus. Modalism was certainly one such belief that did irritate the misunderstanding Tertullian party. It is important to realize that before the reactionary theologizing of these trinitarian church leaders, there was no such concern, in all previous redemptive history, about a complex makeup to the Godhead.

Since we do not have, in our modern era, the apostles of the Lord Jesus to instruct the church in pure doctrine, we must resort to the only authoritative means that remains for us to learn the divinely revealed truth for the church's faith—the canon of inspired scripture. We cannot look confidently to the uninspired theological speculations of the subsequent church leaders since the apostolic era. *We must look past theologians to the inspired writings themselves for our learning,* as well as our unlearning of errors. But even then, we must be careful to look at the inspired writings in their true historical progression and context in order to gain a sound perspective. *The Hebrew prophets have the priority of revealing the nature and plans of God, and then the apostolic writings confirm and elucidate their messages.* If this order is not respected, then there will be errors, as in fact there are.

Some skeptical New Testament theologians, who would deny the deity of Jesus (as the God-man, in my understanding) as a held belief since the apostolic era and would claim it was an invention of the nascent church, make the mistake of examining only the circumstances of the New Testament while failing to consider the Old Testament prophecies concerning the coming Messiah. The ground of our evangelical Christian belief in the deity of Jesus does not begin with the New Testament but rather with the Old Testament. Therefore, we will begin where the revelation began—with Moses and the Hebrew prophets.

There are two controlling principles which must be kept in mind when examining the scriptures concerning any doctrinal conception. And these principles apply throughout both the Old Testament and the New Testament since they comprise the one progressive and purposeful revelation of the God of Israel. The first principle is that the Torah document (the Pentateuch comprised of Genesis through Deuteronomy, and perhaps including Joshua, making a Hexateuch) is the foundational revelation, and all the later scriptural developments of the Hebrew prophets were both influenced and bounded by the Torah disclosures concerning the character, the will, and the redemptive purposes of God. We know this because nothing prior to God's grace to Abraham and his descendants in Israel are recalled for the prophetic exhortation toward repentance and commitment toward God. There are many scriptural examples (Gen 26:1–5; Gen 28:10–15; Gen 32:9; Gen 35:9–12; Gen 50:24; Exod 2:24; Exod 32:13; Ps 77:11–20; Ps 105:5–11, 42; Ps 147:19–20; Isa 63:7–16; Jer 2:5–8; Dan 9:11–13; Hos 11:1; Mic 7:14–20). Then the second principle follows naturally from the first in that the apostles of the Messiah Jesus taught nothing but what was previously revealed through those commissioned prophets, doubtless with inspired insight by the Holy Spirit (Luke 1:54–55; Luke 1:68–73; Acts 26:22; Rom 1:1–2; 1 Pet 1:10–12).

We will examine the nature of the Godhead according to the canonical scriptures and in the textual form as we have received them by God's providence. That is, though there may in fact be layers of redaction by various writers of the scriptural books stemming from later periods of time than the contents of the books themselves are recounting, still the textual matters are logically and necessarily concerned with a linear order of progressive revelation and an organic development of narrative. They are incorporated by God's providence.

The covenantal relationship that God had established with the Israelites was essentially a calling to know him truthfully and to serve the only true God, and so necessarily required that God's full nature be disclosed to those who were called out of the darkness of idolatry in order that they might fulfill the Sinai contract. There was no reason for God *not to reveal* his whole nature, or the complete makeup of his Godhead at that critical juncture, contrary to some trinitarian apologists, which we will examine. If the Father seeks such worshipers who were to know him rightly, then he must be known accurately and fully, else they would not have a true conception of him. When we read of the pleasing and justifying faith of the godly ones, such as Abel, Enoch, Noah, Abraham, Moses, and David, there is no sense perceived in scripture that they had an inadequate knowledge of God but rather it was of the same essential content that the New Testament believers possessed.

We will see that the revealed knowledge of God's nature remained constant throughout the biblical epochs but that his plan of redemption progressively unfolded. The prophets expanded upon the Torah revelation but added no new feature of God's nature. All of the nature of the Godhead was already fully revealed during the Mosaic covenant. For God to only partially reveal the nature of his spiritual makeup at Sinai (supposing it was more complex) would certainly provoke confusion and distrust at a later period of full disclosure; and if that later period is the coming of the Messiah then such an apprehension would cast a shadow of distrust over the previous general revelation of God and his purposes. A new religion would have been introduced.

Perhaps the best evidence that the nature of the Godhead is unitary, and not complex, is the fact that the Holy Spirit of God (which is supposed to be the third member of the Trinity) had already been revealed and known as early as God the Creator himself had been known during the formative patriarchal and Israelite interactions, and yet *there is nowhere to be found that Israel regarded the Spirit of God as a distinct person from Yahweh himself.* This is proved by the facts that the Spirit is not distinctly addressed, nor distinctly praised, nor distinctly prayed to, nor is there communication between God and his Spirit as between two persons, nor is it mentioned in Israelite worship as an accompanying member of the Godhead. Even after several centuries during which the Israelites possessed the awareness of the Holy Spirit, at least in their sacred scriptures, the later prophets did have a distinct knowledge of the Spirit of God but they share no perception that he is a person distinguishable from Yahweh. It was still regarded as the interactive presence of God himself (Neh 9:20, 30; Isa 63:7–14). In fact, so unknown was the concept of the Trinity in the nascent church that there is recorded the experience of Paul encountering new disciples who had not even heard of the Holy Spirit! And Paul does not bother to inform them of the supposed trinitarian understanding but is only concerned with which baptism they had received when they had believed the gospel (Acts 19:1–7). These basic facts regarding the Spirit are to be seen in both the Old Testament and the New Testament consistently.

Another significant evidence is the fact that God had *manifested himself in the material form* of a man or an angelic messenger many times already throughout the Torah narrative. Clearly, God assumed real human nature in some situations where he even could eat real food or wrestle with another man, as he certainly did with Abraham and Jacob respectively (Gen 18:1–8; Gen 32:24–26). These accounts constitute an unambiguous demonstration of God's willingness and ability to condescend to the order of humanity for the purpose of real participation. These amazing theophanies are in fact real but temporary incarnations of God. These particular divine appearances in the form of a created nature actually provide evidence that the Hebrew Bible is already familiar with the Christian idea of God becoming a man for the closest possible relationship.

The reality is that both ideas of the Spirit of God as his local presence only and the incarnation of God as a man are discovered in the Old Testament centuries before the coming of the Messiah. However, there is no biblical evidence that these varied manifestations of the one true Deity were ever considered by ancient Israel as disclosing several members of a complex Godhead, each being co-essential, co-eternal, and distinct from one another. It is therefore absurd and dishonest for church theologians to assert that there was a complex nature of the Godhead finally and fully revealed with the clarifying advent of the Messiah Jesus and the pouring out of the Spirit on the new church. These phenomena, at least in principle, were already known long before in the Jewish community but without the freakish interpretations that are incompatible with the Torah revelation of the nature of God.

The Spirit of God is regarded by the Hebrews, even as God himself demonstrates, as an extension, or a mode, of the *presence* of God during his interactions with the created world or men in particular. It is his localized personal presence, while in another sense he is amazingly omnipresent otherwise. The very language employed by God in the scriptures recounting the dispensing activity of his Spirit is more appropriate for describing the idea of his felt influencing presence rather than the giving of a supposed member of the Trinity. It is far more understandable that God can personally interact with many of his servants simultaneously around the world than to think that he "gives," "pours out," "sends" a distinct personal member of the Godhead. Such language seems unworthy of the Spirit if he really is co-equal to the Father, as though he were a servant or a substance rather than the Deity.

Therefore, since the Spirit of God was already known but not considered to be a distinct personal member of the Godhead from the earliest revelation, then the assertion that the later introduction, during the New Testament epoch, of the Son of God (the other supposed member of the Godhead) as an eternally distinct person is not at all believable. The reason being that if the Spirit is not divinely introduced to Israel as a distinct member of the Godhead while he is already known by divine interactions, then the later conception of the Trinity is shattered. The Trinity idea is already broken before the coming of Jesus. To this day, the Jews have never regarded the Spirit as a distinct person from Adonai but only as an extension of his presence in a localized manner, as do Moses and the Hebrew prophets.

The trinitarian apologetic notion that the Spirit, considered as a member of the Trinity, was only scripturally intimated here and there during the biblical period is absurd because there simply is *no satisfying reason* that can be offered by them as to why God would adopt such a hesitant manner of disclosure of his complete makeup. The silly explanation by some of the early church fathers—that Israel might have been tempted to idolatry if the Trinity were fully disclosed—is dismissible when we see how one supposed member was already disclosed, and also how prone to idolatry Israel was even without the complete disclosure. Its absurdity is confirmed when we realize that neither the later prophets nor the apostles employ those few puny "intimations" as proof-texts for teaching the doctrine of the Trinity even when it was supposed to be fully disclosed since the coming of the Messiah Jesus.

Finally, in my opinion, the dogma of the Catholic Trinity is demonic. It renders many otherwise fine teachers of biblical theology to be dishonest and stupid in their hermeneutical ability to look at this doctrinal matter, thereby perpetuating doctrinal impurity and volatility. Satan always seems to come to the argument with his "Did God really say?" whenever I present the very words of Jesus. It makes many trinitarians arrogant, defensive, mocking, unhumble, and unable to look honestly into the matter. Sometimes it makes them immediately consign to hell the one who dares to question this dogma, and then drives that one from fellowship. When a fellow Christian does not really care that Jesus plainly confesses that "only the Father" knows him, or that "I and the Father are one," or that "I am in the Father and the Father is in me," or that "If you really know me, you will know my Father as well," or that "Whoever hates me hates my Father as well,"—which verses express Jesus delimiting the divine worship to two persons—but that Christian pretends that the Trinity is always implied by Jesus, then that dogma is demonic. That Christian does not care what Jesus has really said. They make Jesus a liar. Indeed, they make Moses a liar, who never taught Israel to worship the Spirit. They make Paul a liar, who taught that the church has only God the Father and the Lord Jesus Christ for her Deity. They make God a liar, who knows of no other God beside himself. It also keeps the Jews from being attracted to the gospel of Jesus Christ because the trinitarians present his salvation on a freakish platter rather than the glorious heritage of Moses and the Hebrew prophets.

1

Abraham

THE TORAH PORTION OF the Hebrew Bible is comprised of the five books of Moses, Genesis through Deuteronomy. At the early stage of the Torah narrative, an event is recounted that will have an extremely important impact on the progressive revelation given by God concerning the plan of redemption, which will also demonstrate an important aspect of the character of God's love for the humanity that he wills to save. After the fall of humankind by the sins of Adam and Eve in the garden of Eden, God pronounces not only punitive curses but also the surprising announcement of rescuing grace. This spiritual redemption will be *through the agency of a descendant* of Adam and Eve, through the involvement of employing a human being in the plan of restoring humanity to the right relationship with God their Creator. This divine determination to help defeated mankind is pre-figured by the natural animosity between humans and snakes, but the victory is particularly intimated in the statement that "he (the human male descendant) will crush [the serpent's] head" (Gen 3:15).

Though it is God's own saving determination, it will not be accomplished, as it were, merely from a distance by his remote influence of grace from heaven transforming sinful men. Rather, there will be provided a human savior upon earth, raised up in due time. However, at this early stage the details of his redeeming actions had not yet been disclosed. This redemptive detail of a human victor demonstrates the amazing kindness of God in desiring to be *closely united* to the humanity that he will rescue, which will be seen to be more than the closeness that was enjoyed by Adam and Eve before sin. Later, the Hebrew prophets will reveal the further detail of God being incarnated in this human savior, permanently, and living among men as one of them.

In the course of time, after many centuries of fallen man's morally darkened and miserable attempts at civilization, God determined to save a people. In the exercise of sovereign, free grace, God acted in history to pursue a portion of sinful humanity for himself by redeeming the Hebrews from the curse and condemnation of his offended holiness (Deut 32:8–9). God did this by providing the means for their enabling to live to his honor in righteousness and true civilization. This invaluable blessing of spiritual reconciliation was in fact a *unilateral* covenant given by God to Abram. God also changed his name to Abraham. God would from now on be committed to blessing Abraham and his descendants with a genuine spiritual relationship. This most valuable component of the covenant of grace would be that *El Shaddai* would be Abraham's God *in real intimacy*, and Abraham and his descendants would be God's people *in real intimacy*. This is the most precious blessing of the covenant as it is repeated often throughout the Old Testament (Gen 17:7–8; Jer 30:22; Ezek 11:20; Ezek 14:11; Ezek 36:28; Ezek 37:27). This divine commitment is the driving force by which God will also eventually cause reconciliation to be realized by his power in the future nation of Israel along with the gradual increase of his kingdom among the Gentiles (Gen 12:2–3; Gen 22:18; Isa 2:2–4; Isa 9:7; Isa 42:1; Rom 11:25–27). This power also produces the faith and obedience that are naturally required in individuals to enjoy this blessedness of intimate fellowship with God (Ps 110:3; Jer 31:31–34; Ezek 36:26–27), and it will be by this same power that God causes the salvation of the wider nation of unfaithful Israel (Deut 30:1–10).

The covenant of grace, which included both spiritual reconciliation and also the land of Canaan (Gen 17:7–8), was decidedly given to the Hebrews who were descended from Abraham. Abraham was formerly a pagan citizen from the ancient Mesopotamian region who was surprised with God's call and the attending transformed heart to leave his father's household, kindred, and country. He was to be blessed with a true spiritual relationship with the one true God and to generate a family of his own who would also enter into this divine calling to be God's own people among the many peoples who did not know or serve him (Gen 18:18–19). Though the covenant pertained to all of Abraham's physical descendants, only a small portion of the children of Israel enjoyed a real intimacy with God because of the sovereign selective application of the spiritual circumcision of the heart, which is later disclosed through the ministry of Moses (Deut 30:6; and see Exod 33:19). This unilateral, sovereign grace is absolutely necessary in the making of a real child of

God, as will be seen more clearly in later scripture through the ministry of the apostles of the Messiah Jesus (Rom 2:28–29; Col 2:11).

It was at this most important juncture that God (known then as *El Shaddai*), in his mercy, declared to Abraham the desire to give a covenant to him and his descendants. It was then that God transformed his heart by spiritual circumcision, producing the loving reliance known as "faith," and entered into a real relationship with Abraham. Abraham responded reverently and trustingly to the call of God upon his life, and he was graciously and freely counted "righteous" because of this trust in the revelation of God (Gen 15:6). This divine grace that makes the soul alive to the real God was undeserved and unasked by the moon-worshiping pagan but was certainly received by Abraham, and the command obeyed, because of the necessary transforming grace that rendered his heart willing to respond favorably to the divine calling. This critical and necessary supernatural influence, which is always sovereignly initiated, would be progressively revealed through the ministries of Moses and the later Hebrew prophets of God, and further affirmed by the apostles of the Messiah Jesus.

This calling event required both a spiritual departure as well as a social departure from Abraham's former ungodly environment. He first had to renounce, in his heart, his former mistaken perceptions about the spiritual realm and the nature of deity which he inherited from cultural traditions, and then had to leave the relatives and society which were in fact the strong invisible props to these deceitful perceptions. This significant repentant departure from his former life and the embracing of the true God (including the realization of his true nature) was a kind of crossing-over; and so, he and his descendants are then called "Hebrews." The word comes from the Hebrew term *abar,* which means to "pass" or "cross over."

This event of Abraham's repentant response to God's commandment to enter into a genuine relationship with himself is fundamentally a type or picture of the profound conversion that takes place when God determines to save a person from their lost condition. Such a graced person is rescued from living and feeding upon lies and fictions of both false deities and vain philosophies of life's purposes. Abraham in this event becomes a figure of all future individuals who also believe the truth of God's sole reality and prerogatives over mankind. He is regarded as the "father" of all the believing ones in the redemption provided by God's mercy, and so those who do believe are regarded as the sons and daughters of Abraham (Rom 4:11–12). More than this, Abraham's conversion represents the beginning formation of the community of restored humanity to their true God, the beginning gathering of God's portion of humanity, which involves the disclosure of his true nature to his redeemed people. This disclosure is necessary for both a correct knowledge of God and to reject pagan deceptions.

The most important truth that is impressed upon the redeemed person is the true nature of the only real God, who has been insultingly violated by the pagan's life-long embracing of those evil traditions found in whatever particular culture he has been born into. This person will then forsake his inherited traditions and will submit himself to God. This crossing-over, similar to Abraham's, must take place, or one does not become a genuine servant of God. When Abraham encountered God at Ur and also at later stations in his life, fundamental aspects of God's nature were revealed.

We learn that God, the only real and living God, is unknown to sinful mankind so that he was not ever perceived and depicted by any idol-concept. He is invisible and estranged because he is holy, and man is unholy; there is no affinity between God's righteous character and their unrighteous character. He is only known whenever he reveals himself to someone, and then not without changing that person's character first so that he can rightly appreciate God's glorious nature. Abraham did not know God until he was approached by God. Rather, he was a depraved idolater, as all of pagan mankind, and had to be supernaturally redeemed from his own lost condition (Josh 24:2–3; Isa 29:22).

We also learn that God is the only real sovereign deity over the earth so that he has no difficulty promising to give land to Abraham and his descendants (Gen 13:14–17). The supposed gods of these pagan lands and their peoples are fictional and so cannot thwart God's determinations. Later, during the revelation given through the ministry of Moses, this spiritual fact of the solitary being of Yahweh as the only deity in the world will be pronounced more clearly to the redeemed nation of Israel.

We then learn that the person to whom God commits himself to be in relationship with will also have God as that redeemed person's protection, or "shield." God will ensure the good things that were promised to Abraham, and so by his divine power be the guarantor of "reward" for trusting and serving him (Gen 15:1; and see Deut 33:29; Ps 33:20; Ps 115:9; Mic 7:20).

In Genesis 15:6, we learn the critical fact that God will justify the existence of the person who believes, with loving reliance, the revelation of his divine person, will, and promises. This free justification of one's moral person will be purely by grace, and be given as a gift of grace and not according to personal merit, which no one can claim as a sinner. Abraham was freely considered righteous simply because he trusted in God's words to him. This dispels any notion that a man can be considered righteous according to God's moral standard and to be accepted into God's holy presence merely by one's personal efforts of right living. This will hold true even for those who were brought under the grace of the Mosaic covenant, who were to be considered righteous because of love and faithfulness toward Yahweh, and this same love and faithfulness were to be the believers' response in return for the grace of enjoying a redeemed relationship with Yahweh as a covenanted people. The expectation of faith in the form of the response of loving and trusting reliance can be seen throughout the Torah (Exod 4:5; Exod 14:31; Num 14:11; Num 20:12; Deut 1:32; Deut 9:23; Josh 1:5–9).

We learn that God is holy in character and separate from sinful humanity, and therefore requires a different lifestyle that will be pleasing to him, which requires a forsaking or repenting of the former lifestyle that did not honor him (Gen 17:1–2). Abraham was commanded to "walk before" God faithfully and be blameless; that is, to live consciously in the sight of God in order to honor him always and with complete integrity.

We learn that God sovereignly chooses whom to give his redeeming love to, and the necessary grace to respond favorably to his election, because he selected only Abram and none of his family members to enter into his covenant (Deut 4:32–38; Deut 7:6–8; Josh 24:2–3, 14; Isa 29:22).

So far, very little was demanded of Abraham for him to fulfill his obligation to the covenant God had given to him. Not many requirements were commanded but that he begin to obey God's surprising directives and to behave himself as if in the presence of God so as to honor him. Abraham was gradually made to experience not only that *El Shaddai* was the true God, but that he had perfect control over destiny, that he required an honoring walk of life before him, and that he was to be trusted as the guarantor of blessing for serving him.

But then a rather surprising aspect of God's nature was disclosed when God appeared to Abraham in the guise of a man. Evidently, God assumed the appearance of a real man temporarily while he visited Abraham at the great trees of *Mamre* (Gen 18:1–33). God was accompanied by two other men in appearance who were in fact angels, and who later departed from God and went toward Sodom (Gen 18:22; see Gen 19:1). The two men also spoke of God's intentions as *El Shaddai* was distinct from themselves (Gen 19:13). But not only did *El Shaddai* himself appear incarnate as a real man who ate food from Abraham, evidently the two men also were incarnate angels who appeared to be very much human to Lot who wished to provide them safe lodging, and who appeared as well to the men of Sodom who thought they were ordinary men to be enjoyed sexually (Gen 19:1–5).

Contrary to rabbinic or Talmudic superstition, their Torah is unashamed to reveal the fact of the willingness of the Creator of the world to approach mankind so closely as to assume a similar, physical form. He did so in order to "walk" in the garden with Adam and Eve, or to appear as an ordinary visitor to Abraham's tent and eat a meal with him (Gen 3:8; Gen 18:1–8). These theophanies were indisputable temporary incarnations of God, some of which were clearly indicated by the inspired text as unmistakable physical modes (Abraham's food is eaten, and Jacob would not let the wrestled man go), and therefore had set the precedent for the future permanent incarnation of God in the predestined Messiah of Israel.

This particular appearance of God to Abraham was remarkable condescension and divine kindness. God desired to show human-like friendship, even to eat a meal with Abraham (Gen 18:8). Having a meal with someone is a basic and universal expression of acceptance and fellowship. God must have assumed somehow a real human form so as to be able to genuinely eat a meal served by Abraham. God also showed great forbearance and friendliness in allowing himself to be dissuaded from sovereign actions that would appear to Abraham as unjust and so inappropriate for the Judge of all the earth (Gen 18:25).

The Torah recounts another theophany in which God appeared a second time to Hagar, the slave-girl of Abraham and Sarah, after Sarah drove her out of Abraham's household (Gen 21:9–21). Again, God himself, as the "angel" of God, spoke of how he would make a great nation from Ishmael (Gen 21:17–18). In the account in Genesis 16:1–16, the appearance of God to Hagar, the slave-girl of Sarah, was evidently in a material form again as the "angel of the LORD" (vv 7, 9). This appearance was a real theophany, and not merely an angelic being, because according to Hagar she was visited by God himself who spoke to her of his determination to bless her offspring also (v 10). Hagar then praised God as the one who saw her distress and had compassion on her (v 13). She was compelled even to name God as "a God who sees" (v 13). She also knew that she was privileged to see God as an angelic being (v 13).

In Genesis 14, we have an important witness to the theological beliefs of Abraham concerning the Godhead. Years before the near-sacrifice of Isaac had taken place, there is the story of tribal warfare and of the rescue of Lot, Abram the Hebrew's nephew. After Abram's victorious battle and the recovery of stolen goods, and of Lot, and of the women and other people, he was met by Melchizedek the king of Salem (v 18). Melchizedek was "priest of God Most High." The Hebrew language is: *vahu cohen lael alyon.* Melchizedek, as priest, blessed Abram, saying, "Blessed be Abram by God Most High, Creator of heaven and earth. And praise be to God Most High, who delivered your enemies into your hand" (vv 19–20). We see several important theological truths in this stated blessing. Melchizedek confessed that there is a God who is most high above all other supposed gods, who is the lone Creator of heaven and earth. Abram accepted this praise of God.

Then Melchizedek praised God who controls all of humanity. Abram accepted this praise of God. We know this to be true because Abram identified Yahweh (*El Shaddai*) as the same God Most High as the Creator of heaven and earth (v 22). Also, Abram honored Melchizedek by giving him a tenth of everything (v 20).

Abraham believed that there is only one God who is most high, that God created everything alone, and that God controls humanity. We know that Abram and Melchizedek jointly regarded God as a single person Being because the Hebrew language expresses God with the singular *El* rather than the plural *Elohim*. The Hebrew verb forms are also singular. It is important to notice that neither of them had an awareness of God being complex in his Godhead.

Finally, we learn that God is concerned for his honor in that he should have sincere and thoroughgoing reverence for his kindness in covenanting to bless those whom he calls into fellowship with himself. This natural concern is seen in God's prerogative to test the quality of devotion that he finds in those who are called to partake of his covenant (Gen 22:1–19; Exod 20:20; Deut 8:2; Deut 13:1–3; Ps 11:4–5).

In Genesis 22:1–19, after God had fulfilled his promise to Abraham, that the aged patriarch would yet have a son with Sarah, and he had fathered Isaac, Abraham was then tested for the sincerity of his obedience and devotion to God. Abraham was commanded to offer up his beloved and unique son Isaac as a sacrifice. The challenge being that not only was this unnatural to parental feelings (v 2) but that Isaac was his only son who could generate the many descendants and so fulfill the promises of God (vv 17–18).

What is extremely important to notice in this *Akedah* event that provides a strong argument for the Jewish Christology is the fact of *God's aloneness in the swearing of an oath before Abraham* in reward for his obedience to the command to sacrifice his uniquely-begotten son Isaac. That is, when Yahweh wishes to swear an oath to assure the realization of his divine intention to bless Abraham, he must swear *by himself* since there was no one greater to swear by. The angel of the LORD said, "I swear by myself" (v 16). The Hebrew language is clear and always uses singular pronouns and verbs, which says, according to my paraphrasing, "and he said: 'In me, I have sworn, declares Yahweh, etc.' " (*vayomer biy nishbathy neumyahweh*). The writer of the Letter to the Hebrews confirms this significant event in Hebrews 6:13–18 that demonstrates the sublime aloneness of the Majestic God of heaven. He says, "When God made his promise to Abraham, *since there was no one greater for him to swear by, he swore by himself,* etc." (vv 13–14; and see Deut 32:40).

Now, the trinitarian theologians often tell the lie that the three members of the supposed Trinity eternally love each other, and that they also have conferred among themselves about the plan of the redemption of humanity. But the Bible tells us that for Yahweh, who is the Father of Israel, there was no one to swear by. Therefore, the existence of the supposed Trinity is not at all believable, and the trinitarians cannot provide any satisfying reason as to why Yahweh could not find another member of the Godhead to swear by, or at least to asseverate his determination to bless Abraham. If the members of the supposed Trinity can mutually love each other, cannot one swear to another?

This event of the divine command to offer up Isaac as a sacrifice is also very telling because it records a near-sacrifice of a human being for the sake of God. He was to be a "burnt offering" (v 2) which was typically made for sin atonement. This in turn proves that the life of any one person is owed to the Creator who in fact is an offended Deity. It also proves that the sacrificing of animals is inadequate to atone for the sins of humans since God would not have demanded Abraham's son if his animal sacrifices had been sufficient. It also intimates that God can, contrary to rabbinic or Talmudic superstition, require the sacrifice of a human being for the purpose of atonement for sin, which we will see that God did eventually provide in the sacrifice of his beloved and unique servant.

It must be honestly admitted that the God of scripture can require human sacrifice for the sake of his service or for atonement for sin, despite the sensibilities of rabbinic Judaism or their repudiation of the Christian doctrine of the Messiah Jesus laying down his life as a vicarious sacrifice for sinners. The account of the near-sacrifice of Isaac at the command of God dispels any rabbinic objection of blasphemy. Just the recorded event alone proves the realism of the Christian message. This profound disclosure of the *Akedah* event becomes an important *type* prefiguring the self-sacrifice of the Servant of God who was the lamb provided in the place of sinners (Isa 53:6–7; John 3:16; Rom 8:32).

I will here state some thoughts concerning the *Akedah* event in reaction to some modern scholarly interpretations of it. Some would assert that the episode has an etiological nature. That is, the account of Abraham having been prevented by God from sacrificing Isaac was written as an explanation as to why Israel was different from the pagan nations that she encountered who notoriously practiced child-sacrifice. It is a story supposedly explaining why Israel legislated against such an evil practice during the ministry of Moses.

But this interpretation, which actually doubts the historicity of Abraham, is not at all believable for several reasons: Supposing that the nation of

Israel was proud of their religion as being truly noble and loving, why would their chroniclers embarrass the character of their God by crafting a myth that ineluctably involves *El Shaddai* as a god demanding the evil of child-sacrifice to begin with? How is he better than the Canaanite gods? More than this, the real credit of condemning the practice apparently should go to the people of Israel rather than their god. So then, why is he honored at all? The facts are that God, the author of life, can demand human life for the punishment for sin, as he had done with Pharaoh's and the Egyptians' first-born sons; and he can demand the Israelites' first-born sons as a sacrifice for his redeeming actions but had instead required the service of the Levites as a substitute (Exod 11:4–5; Num 8:18). These things do not prove God to be a monster but rather demonstrate both that he is a God to be feared when offended, and also that he is merciful.

It would be almost miraculous to believe, as according to the skeptics who think there are many sources of the Torah narrative woven together over time, that different writers from different periods of time would so cleverly contribute to such an embarrassing account of their unique origins, including other tales of origin such as Abraham's deceit in Egypt and Lot's incestuous involvement with his daughters (Genesis, chapters 12 and 19)! Such shameful episodes actually prove the historicity of the Torah narrative. Only the real events combined with the duty to be truthful in service to God can account for such a preserved heritage. More than this, the historicity of the patriarch Abraham is highly probable because the prophets of Yahweh both acknowledge his actual existence as significant in the origins of Israel, and they—as Yahweh's spokesmen—would not dare to attribute lies to him who affirms as much (Isa 29:22; Isa 41:8: Isa 51:2; Isa 63:16; Mic 7:20).

Abraham's grandson Jacob experienced the divine reiteration of the covenant blessings first promised to the patriarch. In a dream, he saw a ladder reaching from the earth to heaven and the angels of God were ascending and descending on it. God stood above it, possibly in a material form, and pronounced the divine determination to carry forward and fulfill the promised blessings initiated with Abraham (Gen 28:10–15). Jacob did not learn anything new about God's essential nature but continued to know him as his fathers Abraham and Isaac knew him (Gen 31:42; Gen 32:9–12; Gen 48:15; and see Hos 12:2–5).

What is also most significant for our study are certain theophanic episodes that recount Jacob's encounters of God appearing to him, evidently incarnate as a man, just as he had to Abraham and Hagar. When Jacob was leaving his cheating uncle Laban, God appeared to him during a dream in the form of an "angel" but who was certainly God himself because the angel announced that he was the "God of Bethel," where Jacob had anointed a pillar to God's honor. And the vow that Jacob had made at that same time was noted to have been vowed to the angel then speaking to Jacob (Gen 31:11–13). Toward the end of his life, when Jacob was blessing Joseph, he recalled how God had shown love to him by stating that God had been his "shepherd" all his life and had been the "angel" or "messenger" that redeemed him from all troubles. Jacob certainly recognized that God was the angel he had encountered throughout his life because he prayed that the Angel who redeemed him from troubles would bless the sons of Joseph (Gen 48:8–16). Only God can give blessings (Ps 75:6–7). This testimony of Jacob regarding the life-long help of Yahweh refutes the trinitarian fiction that interprets these appearances of God to Jacob as being the pre-incarnate "eternal son of God" of the Trinity. Both Bible Testaments know of only Yahweh becoming incarnate in the man Jesus. The Christophanies interpretation is superimposed by the typical trinitarian circular reasoning.

Another important episode is when Jacob was wrestling with a mysterious "man" at the Jabbok river before he was to meet his offended brother Esau (Gen 32:24–32). The text makes it clear that the "man" was actually God himself and not merely an angelic messenger. Evidently God was incarnated in the form or nature of a man since Jacob was able to physically wrestle with him and recognized the fact that he "saw God face to face," from whom he demanded a blessing, and yet remained alive (vv 24, 26, 30).

The essential historicity of this passage that unashamedly recounts Jacob daringly wrestling with God incarnate is substantiated by the notice of a particular eating tradition of Israelite culture that resulted from Jacob's limp (v 32) and also by the later prophet Hosea (Hos 12:2–5). There is no satisfying reason that could be provided by trinitarians as to why Yahweh would not disclose the existence of an "eternal son" at such a time when he himself was willing to appear incarnate. And to say that this event was an appearance of the "pre-incarnate son of God" is desperate speculation prompted by the misreading of the New Testament.

In the saga of Jacob starting in Genesis chapter 25, there is a brief notice of the patriarch erecting an altar in Shechem where he settled (Gen 33:18–20). He called the altar *El-Elohe-Israel* ("God is the God of Israel"), affirming that God was indeed his God. What is significant is the evidence here that the plural form of *El*, which is *Elohim*, is used as a singular designation and does not ever prove a subtle plurality in the Godhead, as the trinitarians like to claim. Jacob (or even the author of Genesis) clearly intends to equate the plural form with the singular form of *El* without any conclusion that it means to intimate the Trinity. Judging by the context in which it is used, the plural form sometimes does mean multiple gods or even angels. But neither the later prophets nor the apostles of the Messiah Jesus ever read this plural term as evidence for the Trinity.

In the saga of Joseph, Jacob's son by Rachel, found in Genesis chapters 37—50, there is the continued sense that what Abraham had learned about God's true nature is all that Joseph knew, and nothing new or different about the Godhead was revealed. God is the sovereign over heaven and earth and is unaffected by the pagan gods of Egypt or Canaan. He alone controls destinies, and grants favor or calamity. The episode that is significant for our study is in Genesis chapter 41, when Joseph was brought out of the dungeon, which he had been unjustly placed in, to interpret Pharaoh's dream. Joseph asserted that his God can give a sure interpretation to Pharaoh. After Joseph interpreted the dream and also proposed wise policies for the land of Egypt in the event of the coming famine, he was promoted to be a ruler of Egypt.

What is important to notice is the language used by Pharaoh (or even the author of Genesis) in stating the rhetorical question, which literally reads: "Who can be found as this, which has the spirit of a god in him?" (Gen 41:38). Pharaoh recognizes that Joseph is favored with supernatural help to be able to interpret dreams and consequently to predict the future. The Hebrew word employed by the Israelite author is the usual plural generic form for "god" (*Elohim*) referring to the God of Israel, and he probably wanted to give the credit to Yahweh for the sake of his readers. But it is more likely that Pharaoh only meant to say that a deity has enabled Joseph by coming into his person to supernaturally influence him. Or at the most, Pharaoh respectfully meant the God of Joseph according to the Hebrews' religious conviction.

What must be appreciated from this episode is the fact that there is absolutely no sense that the "spirit" of any god was considered as a distinct personal entity from that god which it represented. Rather, the spirit of a god was simply the localized supernatural presence of that god. When a god was considered as "being in" someone, even as the spirit of God was said to be "in him" (in Joseph), this meant that god's very presence itself and not a secondary person emanating from that god. Search where you will, such a notion is never to be perceived in the text of the biblical narrative at all. The concept of a multi-personal god is never entertained until it is conceived in the post-apostolic period in the second century of the church.

Later, during the Christological struggles of the early church, it will be claimed by the trinitarian theologians that the reason the Trinity doctrine was not fully disclosed during the Old Testament period (assuming it was finally revealed during the New Testament period) was that ancient Israel was not spiritually ready to receive such a revelation. The supposed divine concern was that they would misunderstand the Godhead to be tri-theistic rather than tri-une, thereby lapsing into a kind of polytheistic idolatry, since they were surrounded by polytheistic cultures at the time. But that concern is a silly reason for Yahweh not to disclose the full Godhead, if that were God's true essential makeup, since no one knows God except by the power of God.

But the reality is that the author of Genesis demonstrates that the idea of the "spirit" of God (or gods) was already known in their culture. Or even if someone skeptical thinks Genesis was composed much later than the formative period of Israel, still the concept of the Holy Spirit was obviously known to the author(s) in ancient Israel. But the Spirit was never regarded as distinct from God himself since there is no worship or doxology or prayer directed toward the Spirit as considered a separate person from God. More than this, even though ancient Israel never lapsed into worshiping a polytheistic version of Yahweh, she still had adopted pagan gods at times. So, the claim of concern from the early church trinitarians is proven to be a desperate falsehood.

All the narrative of biblical history prior to Abraham assumes the nature of God as *unitary*, and there is no awareness of a complex makeup to his being. However, the famous language of God's creating pronouncement that is recounted at the creation event in Genesis 1:26–31: "Let us make mankind in our image" (v 26), is often cited by church theologians as a proof of the complex nature of the Godhead as opposed to a unitary nature, being found in the earliest revelation of scripture. But it is well known and better explained by the Jews that, according to scriptural revelation, God is here somehow involving the host of angels as his divine council in his decision to create mankind in their shared image of God, since undoubtedly the angels were also created in God's image as they are higher beings than men and women (See 1 Kgs 22:19–23; Job 1:6; Ps 89:5–7; Isa 6:1–8).

This trinitarian assertion will also be seen to be a puny and unimpressive proof when we consider that immediately the writer states, in the very next verse (v 27), that "he" (with Hebrew singular pronoun) "created" (with Hebrew singular verb) mankind according to "his" (with Hebrew singular pronoun) image. This exegetical statement affirming the singularity of God's person supports the idea that it must have been the host of angels then present that were being addressed. The text continues to recount the activity and thoughts of God with singular verbs and pronouns. Even the second account of the creation of man evidences the singular personality of God with the singular verb and pronoun (Gen 2:8). There is no awareness of a complex makeup of God's personhood by the writer of these creation accounts. More than this, the trinitarians conveniently ignore the fact that when the Hebrew language uses a plural form of "make" in the first chapter of Genesis, this determination is delimited and only concerns the creation of *mankind* and not the rest of the world that was brought into being. Therefore, the supposed agency of creation should only regard the man and woman rather than the "all things" that is ordinarily said of the Creator-glory of the divinely incarnate Messiah.

This same phenomenon of God addressing his angelic host (probably in the setting of his royal throne room) can be seen in Isaiah's vision in the temple when God expressed his judicial intentions toward Israel in the presence of both the seraphim and the prophet (Isa 6:1–13). Again, we see that God involved the angels in his decision-making while also stating his intentions as a singular personality: "Whom shall I send?" (v 8). This same divine practice can be seen in the account in 1 Kings 22:19–23, where God asks the council of gathered angels who will entice Ahab into attacking Ramoth Gilead.

It is also important to know that, despite these few verses where the plural pronoun is used (the two passages discussed above and the two others in Genesis 3:22 and 11:7, for which the same explanation applies), throughout the rest of the Hebrew Scriptures there are singular verbs and pronouns ordinarily used in referring to God's personhood. Search where you will, there are no other verses that would seemingly disclose a complex personhood, which is strange if this doctrine is not! More than this, the Genesis 1:26 verse is never employed as a proof of God's supposed tri-une nature by the apostles of the Messiah Jesus. In fact, none of the favorite trinitarian proof-texts are cited by any New Testament author as evidence for this teaching. Contrarily, the apostle Paul protests that from the creation of the world, the invisible things of God's nature—his eternal power and divine nature (his Godhead)—*have been understood and seen through the things he has made* (Rom 1:20).

2

Moses

PSALM 90 IS CREDITED by the Jews to Moses, the man of God. The opening verses are significant for my argument: "Lord, you have been our dwelling place throughout all generations. Before the mountains were born or you brought forth the whole world, from everlasting to everlasting you are God" (Ps 90:1–2). Here, Moses addresses Yahweh as "my Lord" (*Adonai*), using the singular pronominal address "you" (*atah*). Moses also credits the creation of the whole world to him alone. He praises Yahweh as the God with the singular title *El*. After many years of walking closely with God, Moses knew Yahweh only as a single person Deity who created all of the world alone.

In Deuteronomy 34:1–12, the death of Moses is recounted, and in verse 10 he is praised as the exceptional prophet of Israel: "Since then, no prophet has risen in Israel like Moses, whom the LORD knew face to face." The exceptional intimacy that Moses had enjoyed with Yahweh is expressed succinctly with the words "face to face." The Hebrew terms are the plural form of "face" (*panim*) and are used for both Yahweh and Moses. The plural "faces" of Yahweh no more proves a complex Godhead than the plural "faces" of Moses proves a complex nature to the being of Moses. However, the term "face" always proves personhood; and of Yahweh it is said that "he" knew Moses, with the singular pronoun. But we never read that the Spirit of God knew Moses face to face alongside the intimacy of Yahweh with Moses.

The nature of the Godhead of Yahweh was fully revealed by means of divine disclosures as well as the presumptions of the inspired writer during the era recounted in the foundational Genesis narrative, as we have seen. But Yahweh's plan for the redemption of mankind had not yet been fully revealed. Briefly, God's nature consists of being a singular, pure, uncreated, eternal, personal spirit who created and controls all things, who is holy, righteous, just, loving, merciful, blessed, and joyous. He has manifested himself sometimes both as the Holy Spirit in localized encounters and appeared incarnate as a man among men. And during the period of the forthcoming Mosaic covenant narrative there is no sense that God was known by the congregation of Israel to be any different than what the Hebrew patriarchs had previously learned. This fact is evidenced by the beliefs and teachings of Moses during his ministry recounted in the wider Torah narrative.

In the covenant of grace established with the nation of Israel, God continued to be worshiped as a single person Deity without any disclosure of a tri-personal nature within his essence, nor was there any worship or prayer directed toward the Holy Spirit as though distinct from Yahweh himself, and no recognition of a secondary divine person alongside Yahweh construed from the material theophanies. These incarnational appearances never produced, in those who were visited, a conviction of a secondary being distinguishable from Yahweh; but rather, the writer always regarded or named the one who appeared to them as Yahweh himself (Gen 15:2; Gen 16:13; Gen 18:22; Gen 26:24–25; Gen 28:17; Gen 32:30; Gen:35:15; Gen 48:15–16; Exod 3:6; Josh 5:15; Judg 13:21–22). And God himself (who was known as *El*, or *Elohim*, or *El Shaddai* before Moses), or even the inspired writer of the text, revealed that it was he alone as the one appearing to those who were visited (Gen 3:8; Gen 18:1, 22; Gen 22:16; Gen 28:13; Gen 32:28; Exod 3:2–6; Exod 23:20–21; Judg 13:16; Hos 12:3–5). The person of "the angel of the LORD" was consistently regarded by the Hebrew prophets as one and the same as God but in a visible material form (Gen 48:15–16; Isa 63:9; Zech 12:8).

But though God had, in principle, revealed himself to the patriarchs fully, this does not mean all of the descendants privileged to know him had clearly understood that their God was in fact the only real god and therefore all others were inventions. It is clear that the later generations of Jacob's sons had eventually succumbed to local paganism because when they were delivered from Egyptian bondage, they had not heard of the God that Abraham, Isaac, and Jacob had known. Therefore, God had to be newly declared by Moses to the enslaved Hebrews (Exod 3:13–18), and they had to be told to put away foreign gods. And though Jacob undoubtedly reared his children with a knowledge of his redeeming God, still they did not necessarily love God sincerely, as can be seen by their moral character, nor regarded him as the only real god but merely a tribal god among other gods.

At the beginning of the deliverance and formation of the covenanted people of Israel, when they were newly emerging from an idolatrous culture, they were made aware that the God of their fathers would be their redeemer (Exod 3:13–17). However, they probably thought of him as one god among many, but who was mightier, as Jethro exclaimed to Moses (Exod 18:9–11). But after some time of testings and trials, the Israelites were then plainly instructed in the whole knowledge of Yahweh's sole reality, indicated by such language as "the whole earth is mine," and "the LORD made the heavens and the earth," and "the LORD is God in heaven above and on the earth below. There is no other" (Exod 19:5; Exod 20:11; Deut 4:32–40; Deut 6:4–15; Deut 10:14). They were required to fear him alone and to discount any foreign god idea. They were graciously privileged to be made aware of *the spiritual reality of the universe.*

Polytheism was deeply ingrained within the psyche of the ancient world's people-groups and so it was a very normal part of their cultures. They certainly believed the false gods to be real and therefore were physically represented by the crafted idols that depicted them. It was essentially the current life-philosophy or worldview. In our modern times, other worldviews, usually more materialistic, has affected the West. And in the Eastern cultures, there are still more preternatural life-philosophies, including crass idolatry. These worldviews are more or less sincerely believed in, and therefore constitutes the particular spiritual darkness that a convert to the true God must renounce, even as Abraham had done in his own place and time.

According to the Bible, wherever the true God was not known and worshiped, then evil spirits, or demons (*Shadim*), would slyly take God's place and receive the devotion of the pagans (Lev 17:7; Deut 32:17; 1 Cor 10:20). The heathens must have felt at times as receiving actual benefits from the gods they worshiped and trusted in. Evil spirits do seem to have some supernatural powers so as to deceive the devotees, but only by the sovereign permission of God, as in the case of Pharaoh's magicians (Exod 7:11–12). The psalmists seem to recognize how the ungodly pagans revered their own gods as powerful deities, but they themselves were ready to praise the true divinity and glory of Yahweh as the sole creator of the very realms that the false gods were supposed to have created and rule over (Ps 95:3–5; Ps 96:4–5). The pagans believed in their existence and revered them, but the psalmists knew those gods were nothing but imaginary inventions, saying, "for all the gods of the nations are idols" (Ps 96:5).

The covenanted nation of Israel was clearly instructed that Yahweh, their redeeming God, is the only real god in the entire universe and so they were to discard any notion of the real existence of all foreign gods. But this inculcation of the aloneness of Yahweh as God through the ministry of

Moses did not necessarily affect every individual Israelite profitably. After the shameful failure of the national covenant experiment, many in Israel, and then Judah, were condemned by the Hebrew prophets as having secretly or openly worshiped other neighbor gods despite the plain teaching through Moses (2 Kgs 17:7–23). This covenant deviation was particularly mentioned in the song of indictment that Moses was commanded to recite as a witness against Israel's breaking of the covenant (Deut 32:15–22; see also Josh 24:14; Neh 9:18; Amos 5:25–27; Acts 7:39–43). Nevertheless, for the ones that were "circumcised of heart" and feared him sincerely, Yahweh was their only God and Redeemer.

The career of Moses provides several paramount lessons that contribute to our study of the Jewish understanding of the nature of the Godhead, and which also show the experiential convictions about God to which Moses held fast. Moses, as well as the Hebrew patriarchs, experienced the appearing of God to him in a material form (even if angelic), and also experienced the particular sending of the "Angel of Yahweh" to lead the people as an *incarnational* presence of God since Yahweh warns that the Angel was to be obeyed because Yahweh's Name "is in him" (Exod 23:20–21). Moses, as the premier inspired prophet of Yahweh, had encountered both the "Angel of Yahweh" and the "Spirit of Yahweh," but he never concluded that these manifestations of God were to be regarded as evidencing distinct members of the Godhead. Nor did he instruct Israel to worship them as distinct members of the Godhead. But the Trinity dogma makes Moses to be a liar and an unfaithful prophet of Yahweh.

In the book of Exodus, Yahweh had appeared to Moses initially in the form of the "Angel of Yahweh" in the midst of a burning bush that was not consumed by the fire. But then the text clearly reveals that it was in fact *he* himself, and not a mere angel, that had appeared to Moses and that *therefore the ground was holy ground.* Moses reverently removed his sandals and hid his face for fear of looking at God (Exod 3:2–6). Whenever the "Angel of Yahweh" appeared, he demanded reverence. He was to be obeyed as God himself was to be obeyed (Exod 23:20–21); and later, Joshua also was commanded to show reverence because the ground was holy (Josh 5:13–15); and he was honored, as God was to be, by Abraham, Hagar, and by both Manoah and his wife (Gen 16:7–14; Gen 22:11–13; Judg 13:15–23). But whenever mere angelic messengers did appear to men, they did not announce that the ground was holy or required a form of worship. On the contrary, they did not allow such reverence to be shown to them which is only due to the Deity (Rev 19:10; Rev 22:8–9; and see Heb 1:6). Therefore, one of the beliefs of Moses was that Almighty God can, if he wills to do so, assume a human or angelic form and become incarnate. And this was not blasphemous in his mind.

It is extremely important to realize, from this first encounter of Moses with the only true God, what Yahweh had said Moses should repeat to the Israelites: "God said to Moses, 'I AM WHO I AM. This is what you are to say to the Israelites: I AM has sent me to you.' God also said to Moses, 'Say to the Israelites, The LORD, the God of your fathers—the God of Abraham, the God of Isaac and the God of Jacob—has sent me to you. This is my name forever, the name you shall call me from generation to generation'" (Exod 3:14–15). When Yahweh more intimately revealed his name, he used only *singular pronouns* regarding his personal being: "I AM *WHO I AM,*" and "This is *my name* forever." The Messiah Jesus, being the perfect Israelite fulfilling the Torah of Moses, would be sensitive to this precise divine revelation and would never have contradicted this revealed name by suddenly teaching a three-fold name for God such as the suspicious baptismal formula found only once in the Gospel of Matthew. Moses knew Yahweh as a single person Deity, and Moses spoke with him and enjoyed his favor and desired to see his glory alone, even as Yahweh had said to him, "I know you by name and you have found favor with me" (Exod 33:12).

The trinitarians make much of the plural form of the Hebrew term for God, which is *Elohim.* But during the very important disclosure of Yahweh's glory to Moses found in Exodus 34:1–7, Yahweh pronounces his glorious name to Moses and asserts his glorious character to him using the Hebrew singular term for God, *El* (v 6). Evidently, God had no concern to reveal his Being as complex. Rather, this divinely used term strengthens the long-established understanding of the Jews regarding the singular personage of their God and Father. In many places in the Hebrew Scriptures, *El* is used instead of *Elohim.* The trinitarian insistence that *Elohim* implies a complex nature for the Godhead is Gentile ignorance and theological stupidity.

In the book of Numbers, we have a very important account of Moses, which demonstrates his knowledge of the Spirit of Yahweh and how this knowledge did not cause him to regard or worship the Spirit as a separate personage alongside Yahweh within the Godhead (Num 11:4–30). When the people of Israel grumbled against Moses and Aaron, discontented with *manna* and impatient about their lack of delicious food in their journey to the promised land, Moses in turn became discouraged and poured out his complaint to Yahweh how the burden of managing such a people was too heavy for himself. Yahweh then told Moses to select seventy elders to help manage the people. Yahweh said to Moses, "I will take some of the power of the Spirit that is on you and put it on them." (v 17). And when the seventy elders had been enlisted by Moses, Yahweh came down in a cloud and spoke with Moses, and "he took some of the power of the Spirit that was on him and put it on the seventy elders" (v 25). When the Spirit rested on them, they prophesied. The Spirit also rested on two other elders who had not appeared before Yahweh and Moses, and they also prophesied (v 26). Subsequently, Moses expressed the wish that all of God's people would be prophets and that God would put his Spirit on them as well (v 29).

This account shows very clearly that Moses and the congregation of Israel were experientially aware of the phenomenon of the manifestation of the Spirit of Yahweh and its activity. This account also shows the supernatural enabling produced by the presence, or participation, of the Spirit of Yahweh, which can cause any man to serve God rightly. The Hebrew language expresses this statement in verse 17 about the sharing of the Spirit literally, in my translation, as, "I will set aside from the Spirit which is upon you and set (it) upon them," (*va-atsalty min-haruach asher aleykha vasamty aleyhem*). The Hebrew language here does not employ the pronoun "he" or "him" when referring to the Spirit because Yahweh was regarding his Spirit as an attribute of himself, which is not a separate personal being distinct from himself. The Spirit is Yahweh's special presence. Yahweh was "taking some of," or *portioning,* his powerful presence to be upon more persons than Moses. It is absurd to think of a person as portioned out *per se*. But the spiritual presence of God can, somehow, be sent everywhere (Ps 139:7–10). God can, somehow, live in the heart of every Christian believer simultaneously (1 Cor 6:19). It is a mysterious fact of revelation. And the power of that divine presence can be shared everywhere. This is probably how we are to understand the portioning of the Spirit which was upon Moses. God's presence would be attending the seventy elders, and some of that enabling power would be theirs as well. This is probably how we are to understand the "double portion" of Elijah's spirit too, recorded later in the Hebrew Bible.

However, what is more important to perceive from this account is the fact that though Moses knew of the Spirit of Yahweh and its activity, he was *never compelled* to regard the Spirit as a separate person alongside Yahweh—to be reverenced as another member of the Godhead. And Yahweh *never commanded* Moses and the people to regard and worship his Spirit as a separate person from himself. Moses never prayed directly to the Spirit when asking for assistance, nor did he ever directly thank the Spirit for powerful help in his ministry. Later, in the New Testament, we will see this behavior of disregard was consistent in the life of the church.

What is significant about the Mosaic revelation of the Godhead is the stress on his *aloneness*. God, now known as Yahweh, is the only real and living God in all the universe. There is no other god beside him. The gods of the pagan nations surrounding Israel are imaginary. Yahweh existed alone prior to all of the creation of the universe and is completely separate from it. Yahweh plainly declares that he *owns all of heaven and earth and controls all human destinies* (Exod 9:29; Exod 19:5; Exod 20:11; Deut 4:15–20, 32–40; Deut 6:4). All of humanity is dependent upon and answerable to him alone.

In Deuteronomy 6:4–5, Moses gave the essence of *what he believed* and what was required of Israel in the summary pronouncement of the Israelite *Shema*. Moses believed in the revelation of God that he, Yahweh, is the only God who deserves the supreme love of those in covenant with him. The *Shema* asserts that Yahweh, being their God, is "one" (*echad*). Contrary to the false claim of the trinitarians, both Hebrew terms *echad* and *yachad* can ordinarily mean either a singularity or a composite unity, and *echad* is sometimes used to denote aloneness. This sense of aloneness is confirmed by the plain assertions of Moses to the people of Israel that Yahweh is God and "beside him there is no other" (Deut 4:35). This interpretation is also confirmed by the encounter of Jesus with the Jewish teacher of the Law in Mark 12:28–34. The teacher affirmed the *Shema* quote of Jesus as being the greatest commandment and then elaborated that the *Shema* assertion of the Lord being "one" means that there is no other god beside him. The *Shema* continues with the greatest commandment required of the covenanted community. Israel was commanded to love Yahweh their only true God with all of their heart, etc. Israel was to take this fact to heart so as to sweep away their prior misunderstanding of the preternatural realm. Israel, like Abraham, was to experience their own crossing-over from the darkness of paganism to the light of God's reality.

In the *Song of Moses* recounted in Deuteronomy 32:1–43, we read of another significant belief of Moses regarding the glory of Yahweh. This conviction was divinely inspired along with the fact of Yahweh's aloneness as the Sovereign over creation and his deserving of supreme love. This knowledge regarded Yahweh's role as the divine, supernatural "Father" of the nation of Israel. Yahweh is the God who "fathered" them by "creating" them, "making" them, "forming" them (v 6). Earlier, when Moses first received his commission, Yahweh revealed his covenant name and also revealed his "fathering" of the nation of Israel, saying, "Israel is my firstborn son" (Exod 4:22). In the Song, Moses emphasized with the heaping of terms how true and important it was for Israel to know the "fathering" of Yahweh regarding their existence and blessedness. They did not make themselves. It was the grace of their God. This significant disclosure teaches two very important truths: That no one is made a child of God's grace except by God's sovereign pleasure (see Exod 33:19; Ps 65:4); That Yahweh had revealed himself to be known as the "Father" of the children of God (see Deut 14:1). This revelation was important for the people of God. That Yahweh is the heavenly "Father" is a fundamental conviction by which the children of God can revere him correctly with humility, gratitude, trust, and love.

In the minor prophet book of Malachi, we have more evidence for the Hebrew prophets' regard of the Fatherhood of Yahweh as the Creator and Protector of Israel. Malachi knows and speaks for Yahweh as the single personage Almighty God who formed and loved the sons of Jacob as the prophet delivers his dreadful rebukes for the people's renewed covenant unfaithfulness. Yahweh is both the Father and the Master of Israel and Judah: "'A son honors his father, and a slave his master. If I am a father, where is the honor due me? If I am a master, where is the respect due me?' says the LORD Almighty" (Mal 1:6). Afterward, the prophet begins a rebuke for another matter of covenant unfaithfulness through the cruel divorces and pagan intermarriages taking place. Here, the prophet reminds the people of their common origin with the divine Fatherhood: "Do we not all have one Father? Did not one God create us? Why do we profane the covenant of our ancestors by being unfaithful to one another?" (Mal 2:10).

In Malachi, the prophet knows of only the single person Yahweh who is the Father of Israel. No Trinity is acknowledged or honored. The Holy Spirit is never mentioned. And whenever God speaks of himself, it is as a single personage: "*I have loved you*" (Mal 1:2); "It is you priests who show contempt for *my name*" (Mal 1:6); "*My name* will be great among the nations" (Mal 1:11); "'For *I am a great king*,' says the LORD Almighty, 'and *my name* is to be feared among the nations'" (Mal 1:14); "*I the* LORD do not change. So you, the descendants of Jacob, are not destroyed" (Mal 3:6); etc.

The importance of this revelation of the Fatherhood of Yahweh can be seen in the Hebrew prophets. In Isaiah 63:7—64:12, there is a very moving song of praise and prayer for mercy. Recalling the same Torah events of the redemption and establishment of the nation of Israel, the prophet proclaimed Yahweh as their "Father," saying, "But you are our Father, though Abraham does not know us or Israel acknowledge us; you, LORD (Yahweh), are our Father, our Redeemer from of old is your name" (Isa 63:16; and see Isa 64:8). The prophet believed exactly as Moses and Israel believed, that Yahweh's title was "Father" as well as "Redeemer" (see Exod 6:6). This is where Yahweh got the title "Father." Neither of these designations are inherently eternal. These relationship terms began with the historical redemption and establishment of the nation of Israel as Yahweh's covenant people. Yahweh emphasized his founding of Israel as his special glory (Deut 4:32–35; Deut 7:6–8).

The Creator and Protector of Israel was the only sense of the title "Father" by which God was known to the Hebrew prophets. This was also the sense of the title by which God was known to Jesus, the perfect Israelite and

Messiah. This sense of "fathering" Israel is the only possible sense that could be used concerning both Jesus and his disciples. But the sense of "redeemer" or "savior" is not shared with Jesus; at least, not as redeemer from the guilt of personal sin. Later, in the study of the New Testament, we will see in what special sense Jesus called Yahweh his "Father." But the Mosaic sense of the Fatherhood of God was why Jesus taught his disciples to pray "Our Father in heaven" (Matt 6:9; and see Luke 11:2). This is why the apostles of the Lord Jesus, in their New Testament letters, called upon God as "our Father" as well as "the Father of the Lord Jesus Christ." Moses knew nothing, believed nothing, nor taught anything about Yahweh being an "eternal Father" as being due to having an "eternal Son" according to the Catholic Trinity dogma.

Moses never perceived that there was a complex nature to the Godhead, nor that the divine Being that materially appeared to him was to be regarded as a secondary person alongside God, subsisting somehow distinct from Yahweh. Consequently, Moses did not instruct the congregation of Israel about a complex makeup to their Redeemer, nor to worship God as such. The people were acquainted with only a single-person divine Being and were commanded to fear and swear by *his name alone* (consistently stated with singular grammatical construction). Another secondary name was not provided as the object of religious fear and trust. But Moses would have been an unfaithful prophet of Yahweh to neglect such a momentous detail of the Godhead whom the nation was commanded to know and worship by his unparalleled ministry. It is one aspect of the glory of God that he had made known "his ways"—his core moral feelings and sovereign disclosures consistent with these core feelings—to Moses and the sons of Israel (Ps 103:6–8), but why not his full essential nature as a supposed multi-personal Deity, if indeed that is the case?

According to the Fourth Gospel, the Torah document containing the revelatory ministry of Moses "wrote" of the Messiah to come in such a way that the Jews should have perceived his predestined redemptive mission to Israel (John 5:45–47). But there is nowhere to be found in Moses a plain announcement of a messianic purpose in so many words, and certainly not a simple express prediction of the man, named "Jesus," to be yet born for Israel. But Jesus asserted that Moses "wrote" of him. As will be seen later, a careful assessment of the unique contents of the Fourth Gospel, which are not found in the Synoptic material, makes it fairly plain that what was meant was the way the Torah narrative employed various *types,* which foreshadowed the glorious complex role of the Messiah as the "word," a "light," a "lamb," as the "temple," as the "bread from heaven," as the "high priest," etc. This was some of the ways Moses wrote of the Messiah to come. However, all of these things as types are derived from the will of God and *are not*

God himself in themselves, and they have a *derived glory* which served the redemptive purposes of God. But again, Moses did not therefore teach a future revelation of a secondary divine being fulfilling these types. Rather, the apostles will maintain that it was God himself who fulfilled these types in the ministry and person of Jesus being the true substance of these things. These things fulfilled by Jesus were foreshadowed in the Torah narrative— Jesus being the better sacrifice and providing the better priesthood (Col 2:16–17; Heb 7:20–28; Heb 8:6; Heb 9:11–14).

3

The Soul of Yahweh

THE OLD TESTAMENT CONTAINS the complete revelation of the nature of God and his Spirit as understood according to Moses and the Hebrew prophets. In various ways, they have either encountered God personally or have had revelation disclosed to them, which they have recorded in the Scriptures. The primary revelation of God and his will has been providentially documented in the Torah, which is the foundational body of inspired scripture. After the career of Moses, there was yet more interaction between God and his chosen national people, by which various prophets have recorded further narrative that contains important disclosures of his Spirit. Some prophets were anonymous and some we know by name. But all were inspired and provide an accurate record of their encounters, which exhibit the true nature of God.

The most important argument to be understood from this biblical period of the Torah is that we see that the Holy Spirit of Yahweh was already well known and mentioned at certain times by Moses and other members of Israelite society, but the Spirit of Yahweh was never regarded or worshiped as a separate person alongside Yahweh. Rather, Yahweh himself was regarded as a single person, endearingly called the "Father," as will be demonstrated. He was never regarded as a Being with a complex Godhead consisting of multiple personages. In Old Testament scripture, "spirit" is the same as the "soul" or "heart," and sometimes "breath." Also, "heart" is the same as "mind." These are not distinguished from one another in any real sense but are often interchangeable. Yahweh spoke through his prophets of his Spirit using the substitute term "soul." For example, in Psalm 11:5, "his soul" hates the violent man. And in Psalm 130:5, the psalmist says, "I wait" for the Lord, as well as "my soul" waits for the Lord. In Job 33:4, Job states the "breath" (*neshamah*) of the Almighty created him as well as the "Spirit" (*ruach*) of God. In Isaiah 30:1, Yahweh complains of Israel's ungodly plans which, he says, are "not mine" (*velo miny*), which would be the same as "not of my Spirit" (*velo ruchy*) according to the Hebrew parallel poetry in the verse.

However, these facts of the Jewish knowledge of the Spirit of God have not been rightly appreciated for their implications. As a result, there is a poor understanding of the nature of the Spirit of God in our modern era of the Christian church and has been poorly understood for most of church history. The reason is mainly because the church, which became mostly Gentile from the earliest period, had lost sight of the Hebraic (or Jewish) understanding of the Spirit of Yahweh. Therefore, it is extremely important to regain a correct Hebraic definition of the Spirit, which will then help us correctly understand both the nature of the Godhead and the Messiah Jesus.

During the Patriarchal period that is documented in Genesis, the Spirit of God is barely mentioned. It seems that the mode of God's Spirit was first made consciously known by Yahweh to Moses during the formation of the covenanted nation of Israel. Yet Moses never teaches or commands Israel that God's Spirit be, therefore, consciously regarded as a personage distinct from the personage of Yahweh, the Father of Israel. Consequently, there is no directive found in the Torah to fear, praise, or pray to, the Spirit as being separate from Yahweh. The Hebrew prophets which arose and ministered after Moses continued to have both an awareness and experience of the Spirit of God, which are mentioned frequently throughout the remaining biblical period found in the Hebrew Bible, yet without giving praise or directing prayer to the Spirit of God as though it were a separate person to be worshiped. This fact needs to be emphasized and is extremely important to bear in mind going forward in this study.

There are certain events in the biblical narratives and comments in the Psalms involving the Spirit of God that will show us how the Hebrews regarded this particular manifestation of God's Being. I will discuss the more revealing accounts. A close look at these will contribute to the better theological understanding of the Spirit, which will in turn expose the fallacy of the third-member-of-the-Trinity concept. If the correct Jewish understanding of the Spirit had been maintained in the early church, the tragic mistake of trinitarianism would not have developed.

In Genesis 6:3–6, after the sinful fall of the first humans, Yahweh expresses his wearisome disgust with the dishonoring behavior of subsequent humanity. Yahweh says, "My Spirit will not contend with humans forever, etc." The Hebrew language is simple: "my spirit" (*ruchy*). One of the greatest arguments against trinitarianism is the many absurdities that it involves. In our text here, it is absurd to think that Yahweh is stating that the supposed third member of the Trinity alone is wearied from contending with sinful humanity. The only possible sense is that Yahweh's "heart was deeply troubled," as is stated later in verse 6. Again, the Hebrew is simple: "his heart" (*livo*). And the sense is the same as how the Hebrew term is used regarding the inner feelings of sinful humanity in verse 5, "his heart" (*livo*). Now, we would not absurdly conclude that Yahweh's heart was a distinct personage or component apart from his inner self. The whole context of a passage is critical to ascertaining the right sense of the original language within it. Rather, it was Yahweh *himself* who regretted making mankind, and not just a part of him.

In Genesis 41:1–40, there is the account of Joseph and his wrongful imprisonment while serving under the Pharaoh of Egypt. The Pharaoh had a disturbing dream that predicted future events for Egypt, which could not be interpreted by the magicians and wise men found in Egypt. Then the chief cupbearer, who knew of Joseph's ability to interpret dreams, recommended him to Pharaoh. Pharaoh summoned Joseph and he interpreted the king's dream accurately. Pharaoh was favorably impressed and wanted to search for a man who could be placed in the court position to oversee Egypt's agricultural resources to prepare for the coming famine. Pharaoh asked a question which happened to make a significant description: "Can we find anyone like this man, one in whom is the spirit of God(s)?" (*ruach elohim*) (Gen 41:38).

The sense is clearly the idea of the *localized, supernaturally-influencing presence of God*, or a god, to be found in someone. Again, it is absurd to interpret this phrase as having a meaning that is really a theological subtlety known only to the modern abstruse seminarian! Pharaoh, of course, would not have known of Yahweh nor a distinct personage of God known as the Spirit (the supposed third member of the Trinity). But neither does the Hebrew writer of the account, who would have been knowledgeable of the Spirit of God. The fact that Pharaoh speaks the phrase, "God's spirit" (or "a god's spirit"), being in Joseph demonstrates that Pharaoh's understanding of the presence of a deity being able to supernaturally influence a man by direct interaction was obviously the common concept of the ancient culture. Pharaoh would not have known of Yahweh, and so either he just meant the particular deity which Joseph worshiped and served, or he meant the many gods that he himself would have worshiped. But this underscores the common idea of the spirit of a god as being only an extension of its presence, and not a separate personage of that god.

In the book of Daniel, we find a similar episode in which a heathen king needed the help of one in whom was the spirit of the gods which he revered. King Nebuchadnezzar of Babylon had a dream which frightened him, and he was advised to consult Daniel in whom, it was known, "the spirit of the holy gods" was in him (Dan 4:8, and see Dan 5:11, 14). The Babylonians, having no experiential knowledge of Yahweh, merely considered Daniel as being supernaturally influenced by the only gods they would have known. And so they drew attention to him as one in whom was the supernatural abilities effected by the indwelling of the holy gods. The language, which is Aramaic in chapters 4 and 5, makes clear that a plurality of gods is in mind: "spirit of holy gods" (*ruach elohin qadashin*) since the adjective matches the noun in number. This underscores the fact that the Babylonians had an understanding of the quality of the spirit of a god without regarding that attribute as constituting a distinct personage from the named god but was rather the god's personal presence localized.

In Exodus 31:1–11 and Exodus 35:30—36:2, Yahweh is said to have filled Bezalel with the Spirit of God for artistic purposes which were to contribute to the religious furnishings of the tabernacle of Israel. The language is significant and needs to be examined closely. Yahweh said he "filled" (*vaamale*) Bezalel with the "Spirit of God" (*ruach elohim*) (Exod 31:3). Such language does not fit the sacred regard of a deity properly speaking. Are we to think that God pours out the third person of the Trinity as a mere substance, along with other various qualities? This would reduce the Spirit to be less than a servant of Yahweh, something like a substance, and so would not be co-equal in divine majesty. When the writer repeats this divine endowment of Bezalel and others, he simply states that Yahweh endowed them with skill (Exod 36:2). That is, there was no difference between saying the giving of the Spirit of God and Yahweh's giving of skill, because the *direct supernatural influence of Yahweh's presence* is what produced the miraculous skills in their minds. It is one and the same thing.

In Exodus 33:12–17, we have Yahweh speaking with Moses about how God will provide his "Presence" to go with Moses (v 14), saying, "My Presence will go with you" (*panay yelekhu*), which to Moses is the same as he saying to God, "you go with us" (v 16). These are not distinguishable in any real sense. Although the Hebrew term and verb form are plural, Moses never perceives a second personage by this term "Presence," and so never addresses or worships a second personage. It is noteworthy that the term used for "Presence" is the typical Hebrew word "face" (*paneh*), but it is written as a plural, "faces," with the matching plural form of the verb of "go," saying, "they will go" with Moses. We are not to absurdly conclude that there are multiple Spirits of God. Rather, this is the plural of majesty, which is also appropriate where we read the plural term for God, "Elohim," where Yahweh is considered. This significant passage is recounted by the prophet in Isaiah 63:11–14, where it is said Moses and the people were granted rest by the Spirit of God. Now, in the Exodus passage, the rest was given by Yahweh's "Presence." But in the Isaiah passage, the prophet longs for "*he who set his Holy Spirit among them.*" The prophet only longs for Yahweh alone; peace being the benefit of his presence.

In Numbers 11:4–30, the account of the wandering Israelites murmuring and craving for meat, Moses' consequent distress, and Yahweh's solution provides a significant disclosure of the nature of the Spirit of Yahweh. God determined to appoint seventy Spirit-endowed elders to help Moses with the administration of the people. God said to Moses that he will "take some of the power of the Spirit that is on you and put it on them" (v 17; and similarly in v 25). The Hebrew language makes it clear that God is somehow distributing a portion of the same Spirit-influence that enabled Moses to serve God faithfully (*va-atsalty min haruach asher aleykha vasamty aleyhem*). The word "power" is supplied by the English translator, but it is not in the original text. The clause more literally reads, according to my translation, "I will separate from the Spirit which is upon you and place [it] upon them." Are we to understand God saying that he will crudely portion-out the actual distinct person of the Spirit to multiple destinations? This seems to demote the supposed third member of the Trinity to the level of a servant or a substance. Such language does not seem worthy of the personal being of God (if we considered the Spirit as a distinct member of the Trinity, being co-equal in divine majesty), but this expression is appropriate regarding *the presence and power* of God, which can be localized in many places simultaneously.

An evidence that the phraseology used by the biblical authors that describes the distribution of the Spirit as meaning the giving of the localized presence of God for specific purposes is to be found also in the facts that such expressions are *never used* of the persons of God the Father or of the Lord Jesus Christ. These supposed other "members" of the Trinity are never described as "poured out" or "put onto" or one to be "baptized with," *nor are they ever directed* by another member in such a sense, and which intended distributions many times refers to *multiple recipients*. But it is absurd to think that the supposed person of the Spirit can be divided indefinitely to be placed onto many recipients at once. It would be just as absurd to think that the persons of God the Father or the Lord Jesus could be portioned out as a substance! The glorified human body of Jesus cannot be divided, who is now in heaven (Acts 3:20–21). Christ lives in the believers' hearts only "through faith" (*dia tas pisteos en tais kardiais*) through the power of the Spirit (Eph 3:16–17).

Another evidence is in the fact that the bodies of the Christian believers, or the collective congregation, are now the new spiritual temple of God because of the inauguration of the new covenant with the coming of the Messiah Jesus. The apostle Paul uses either expression interchangeably, regarding the believers, that they are "the temple of God," or "the temple of the Holy Spirit" (I Cor 3:16–17; 1 Cor 6:19; 2 Cor 6:16; Eph 2:19–22; see Rev 21:3, 22). But when Paul uses the phrase, "the temple of the Holy Spirit," he is not teaching that Christians are the temple of the supposed third member of the Trinity only, is he?! But consistent trinitarians must conclude this absurdity. If they resort to the explanation that the terms referring to God and the Spirit are used interchangeably, then *they give up their dogma* that asserts the supposed members of the Trinity are "distinct but co-equal." Rather, Paul teaches more clearly that the indivisible, unitary God dwells in the believers *through the medium* of his distributed Spirit, which is his distributed presence, saying, "God's Spirit," and "a dwelling in which God lives *by his Spirit*" (or literally, "in [the] Spirit,") (*en pneumati*) (1 Cor 3:16; Eph 2:22).

It is important to keep in mind that though Moses encountered this manifestation of the Spirit of God being given to certain men, he yet did not regard it as a distinct member of a complex Godhead to be worshiped alongside Yahweh. If he did, he undoubtedly would have been commanded to legislate reverence, praise, and prayer be made toward him also, even as he does command Israel to love and fear Yahweh. The fact is that none of the Hebrew prophets regarded the manifestation of the Spirit of God as evidencing a complex nature of the Godhead in which the Spirit is to be worshiped as a distinct member of that Godhead. As an example already mentioned in Isaiah 63:11, the prophet Isaiah recalls the events of Torah and longingly asks, "Where is he who brought them through the sea . . . Where is he who set his Holy Spirit among them?" Isaiah does not say "where is the Holy Spirit?" but "where is *he* who set his Holy Spirit among them?" He longs for Yahweh himself, who had extended his manifest presence among the people of Israel. If the Spirit of Yahweh was really a separate member of a complex Godhead, then Isaiah would have asked for the Spirit as well. But he asks where is he who had provided his manifest presence among them, which is "his glorious arm of power" (v 12).

This Jewish interpretation, that the Spirit of God is the mode of the localized presence of God rather than a distinct personage, is also supported by the teaching of the apostle Paul in 1 Corinthians 2:10–11. Paul compares the Spirit of God with the spirit of a man. Just as no one knows our deepest thoughts and feelings except our own spirits (or souls), so no one knows the deep things of God except God's own Spirit (or his soul). But a man's spirit is not a distinct entity from himself, so also the Spirit of God is not a distinct personage from God himself. When Paul says that the Spirit "searches" all things of God, he means only that the inner being of God is *thoroughly conscious* of his feelings, thoughts, and plans for the redeemed ones in contrast to ordinary humanity, which is incapable of perceiving the intentions of God toward his servants. In Romans 11:34, Paul chose to quote the Greek Septuagint version of the Old Testament when he quotes the verse found in Isaiah 40:13. There the prophet Isaiah asks, "Who can fathom the Spirit of the LORD, or instruct the LORD as his counselor?" Now the prophet had used the Hebraic idiom of "Spirit" for the heart of God, but Paul substituted the Greek term "mind" from the Septuagint as a proper interchangeable term for "Spirit," providing a good sense, which reads: "Who has known the mind of the Lord? Or who has been his counselor?" *The Spirit of God is the same as the mind of God,* which is not a distinct personage from Yahweh. According to the apostle Paul, the Spirit of God is the soul of God. And if we substituted the term "Soul" in every place that the term "Spirit" is used in reference to God, we would have a better understanding of what the Bible author is saying.

In 2 Kings 2:9, the prophet Elisha asks the prophet Elijah for a double portion of the Holy Spirit that is operating in him. The Hebrew language is more literally, in my translation, "Let it be, please, a double portion of your spirit (*baruchkha*) to me." Again, such language is not worthy of a member of the supposed Trinity, as though the person of the Spirit can be measured as a substance. Rather, this does evidence the measurable supernatural power of the divine presence operating through the ministry of the prophet. More miraculous power can be displayed than what Elijah had shown, just as the Messiah Jesus had said, in John's Gospel, that his disciples would experience the performing of greater works (John 14:12).

According to the Psalmists' employment of the Hebraic poetry of parallelism, the Holy Spirit is the presence of God. God's dwelling and throne are in "heaven" (Ps 11:4; Ps 103:19; Isa 57:15; Isa 66:1). But whenever God wills to directly interact with either creation or mankind, or put forth supernatural power and influence, he condescends and mingles in the mode of his Spirit, which is *the manifestation of his localized presence as opposed to his universal presence.* This is how the Hebrew prophets understood the Spirit. So, David, in his repentance for sin, begs that Yahweh would not cast him away from his presence, which would be done by God removing his Spirit from someone (Ps 51:11).

It is important to notice that David *does not pray to the Spirit directly,* as toward a supposed separate person, begging the Spirit not to leave him. Rather, he prays to Yahweh not to remove *his* presence. It is absurd to think that David is only concerned that a supposed portion of the Trinity would be removed from him. Rather, it is Yahweh himself who dwells with those who fear him (see Isa 57:15). Also, this suggestion does violence to the normal usage of the word for "spirit," which David had just used in the previous verse, speaking of his own invisible inner being as "spirit," which is also his "heart" (v 10). Again, in Isaiah 30:1, by the use of poetic parallelism the prophet Isaiah records the complaint of Yahweh regarding the obstinate Israelites, that they make plans that are "not mine," or more literally, "but not of me," (*velo miny*); and then again says that they form an alliance, but "not by my Spirit" (*velo ruchy*). The clear sense is that Yahweh's Spirit is *his own person,* unitarily understood.

In Psalm 139, the prophet uses poetic parallelism to express his wonder at God's omnipresence, especially in relation to the man whom God loves, according to the statements of care and affection he is recounting in the surrounding verses (see v 10). The prophet asks, "Where can I go from your Spirit? Where can I flee from your presence?" (v 7) The Spirit of God means the presence of God. The ordinary Hebrew term for "presence" is literally "faces of you" (*paneykha*). This term refers to the face of Yahweh and often means his affectionate regard and closeness toward someone who is in covenant with him. It is absurd to understand this comment as regarding only the presence of the supposed third member of the Trinity. When the prophet continues his adoration of God's omnipresence, he further says things that can only be understood of Yahweh himself, such as his creating both the body and the inmost being of the prophet (vv 13–16).

In Isaiah 63:7–19, the prophet discloses a similar evidence of the correct understanding of the Spirit by Hebraic parallelism in the passage of praise recounting the formation of the nation of Israel. The prophet mentions the compassion of Yahweh toward Israel that in all their distress he too was distressed and that the "angel of his presence" saved them (v 9). We must understand that he says, "the messenger of *his* presence." And then further down he says that Israel "grieved *his* Holy Spirit" (v 10). And then consequentially, he, Yahweh, "turned and became their enemy and he himself fought against them." The Hebrew language emphasizes that it was he himself (*hu*) that fought against rebellious Israel. It was not the absurd idea that the supposed third person of the Trinity was grieved and then Yahweh himself reacted with anger, but it was that Israel grieved Yahweh's localized presence which had moved lovingly among them.

Neither the book of Jeremiah nor the book of Lamentations ever mentions the Spirit of Yahweh in any form, though the Hebrew word *ruach* is used for other ideas such as "wind" or "breath." I regard this as practical evidence that the Holy Spirit was not seen as a separate personage by the prophet Jeremiah. It is evidence that he knew nothing of a Trinity. He evidently never perceives that the Torah accounts of the activity of the Spirit of Yahweh disclosed a complex Godhead—whether the creation account or the giving of the Spirit to Moses and other leaders. Jeremiah never gives honor to the Spirit of God as a member of the supposed Trinity. He only addresses Yahweh.

A significant disclosure in the Hebrew Scriptures concerning the ministry of the prophesied Messiah is the supernatural endowment of the anointed man with religious and moral strength of character to fulfill his commission. This supernatural supply is given by the direct influence of the Spirit of God upon his own spirit (Isa 11:1–5; Isa 42:1–4; Isa 49:5; Isa 50:4–5; Isa 61:1–3). In Isaiah 11:2, the text says about the Spirit that "she rested" upon the Messiah. The result is a variety of religious and moral qualities with which he is strengthened for his calling. The term "Spirit" is repeated along with couplings of related qualities in poetic fashion: "The Spirit of wisdom and of understanding, the Spirit of counsel and of might, the Spirit of the knowledge and fear of the LORD." The repeated style does not lend itself to the notion of there being a distinct member of a supposed complex Godhead. Rather, the emphasis is on the manifold qualities that are supplied by the enveloping presence of God upon the Messiah. This must be the correct sense because otherwise the Spirit of God would have to be understood as a female personage based on the use of the feminine verb form, which is not the teaching of trinitarians. And, from a rational perspective, the various spiritual qualities mentioned are in themselves less than a divine personage.

Later, in the New Testament, we will see that this interpretation is underscored by how this poetic description of the multifaceted ministry of the Spirit in Isaiah is utilized similarly by John several times in the book of Revelation. There we read that "the seven spirits of God" are mentioned either before the throne of God, or are in the possession of the exalted Lord Jesus who "holds the seven spirits of God," or are "sent out into all the earth" (Rev 1:4; Rev 3:1; Rev 4:5; Rev 5:6). These expressions cannot sustain the idea of a separate, co-equal member of the supposed Trinity for two reasons: The mention of *seven* spirits of God cannot possibly be referring to the supposed third (singular) member of the Trinity; it is obviously the Hebraic idiom of the number of perfection. The term has the same sense when referring to the candlesticks, which are seven numerically, not seven-fold (Rev 1:20).

The seven spirits are said to be *before the throne* of God—not *on* the throne of God, which means that they are in the *role of service,* and so cannot be the expression of a supposed co-equal divine persona. Any supposed member of the Godhead would naturally be on the throne of divinity rather than before it (Ps 11:4), as we in fact do read of God and the man in whom he is incarnate (Rev 22:1, 3).

The "seven spirits of God" phrase is better understood as expressing the perfect supernatural influence of *the localized presence of God wherever he wills to manifest himself.* It is perfect because the will of God is exactly accomplished in the lives of the redeemed believers. This is why the "seven spirits" are described to be in the *possession* of the Lord Jesus and *sent out into all the earth.* This expression of the mysterious, invisible, distributed presence of God does coincide with the apostolic expressions of the dispensing of the Spirit as though either the material elements of breath, cloth, or water (Mark 1:8; Luke 24:49; John 1:33; John 20:22; Acts 2:33; Acts 10:45).

It is absurd to think that the Lord Jesus, as the supposed second member of the Trinity, disposes the supposed third member of the Trinity as a mere servant. This would be highly inconsistent with their trinitarian statement of co-equality within the Trinity. But it is not inconsistent with the majesty of God incarnate that he would dispose of his supernatural influence as he wills and wherever he wills, as is described by John that "the Lamb had seven horns and seven eyes, which are the seven spirits of God sent out into all the earth" (Rev 5:6).

The Holy Spirit is the localized presence of Yahweh, by which mode he comes from heaven into direct contact with either his created world or men, for the purposes of direct relationships, supernatural influence, and control. For examples, he is the means by which the world was brought into being and sustained (Gen 1:2; Ps 104:30); by which the Hebrew prophets were inspired (1 Pet 1:10–12); by which men are controlled for God's purposes (1 Sam 10:6); by which the heart of man is supernaturally transformed toward godliness (Ezek 36:27; John 3:5–8; 1 Cor 12:3); by which the Christian believer is assured of his adoption by God (Rom 8:16; Gal 4:6); by which the Christian believer is secretly helped with wordless groans of prayer (Rom 8:26–27); by which called men are enabled to preach and minister (Joel 2:28; Acts 1:5, 8; 1 Cor 12:4–11); by which the Christian believer receives grace, peace, and joy (Rom 14:17; 1 Thess 1:6; Rev 1:4); and the very power to live a godly life is regarded as "the fruit of the Spirit," meaning it is *produced* by the supernatural influence of the presence of God in the believer's heart (Rom 8:13–14; Gal 5:22–23). More than this, in 1 Corinthians 2:10, Paul says that the intentions of God are revealed "by his Spirit" (*dia tou pneumatos*). Why would one member of the Trinity need another co-equal member to reveal things to man? Rather, this language evidences the fact that God interacts with men directly through his localized presence.

In scripture, the Holy Spirit is sometimes viewed as an attribute or quality of God's immaterial being. Sometimes the term for "soul" is substituted for "spirit," and this fact also provides mutual exegesis for the idea behind it. This attribute view is when God himself, or the Hebrew prophets, addresses the Spirit using feminine pronouns such as "she," and non-personal pronouns as "it." In the Hebrew language, both the terms "spirit" and "soul" are feminine; and when the Spirit is addressed in the Old Testament as an aspect of God's being, it is designated as "she." In Judges 6:34, it says literally, in my translation, "But the Spirit of Yahweh, she clothed Gideon, etc." In Isaiah 42:1, where Yahweh announces his Servant, God mentions his "soul" and that "she delights" in the Servant.

In the New Testament Greek language, the term "spirit" is a neuter word. The New Testament accounts sometimes employ the non-personal pronoun "it." So, when the New Testament mentions the Spirit as God's personal being and presence, it uses the masculine pronoun such as "he." But when the Spirit is regarded as an immaterial attribute, it is mentioned as an "it." In John 14:17, the Lord Jesus indicates the Holy Spirit as an attribute of God his Father using a neuter pronoun, which the world cannot receive because it "neither sees nor knows it" (*auto*). Again, in John 14:26, Jesus speaks about the Holy Spirit, "which the Father will send in my name, etc." The relative pronoun is neuter. It is significant that with both cases of God's Spirit and man's spirit, the neuter article pertaining to the neuter term of "spirit" (*to pneuma*) is used, which signifies that the spirit is, when considered abstractly, a quality or attribute of a personal being and not a separate personage itself.

Again, the Hebrew term for "spirit" (*ruach*) is a feminine word. Accordingly, the biblical authors of the Hebrew Scriptures frequently use feminine verb forms in the original language texts (Judg 6:34; Judg 11:29; Judg 13:25; Judg 14:19; 1 Sam 10:6, 10; 1 Sam 16:13–14; Isa 11:2), which denote the fact that "Spirit" is the attribute of the extension of God's personal being, the mode of his direct interaction with men and creation. The feminine verb form, which proves the localized presence concept, is underscored in the passage in 1 Samuel 16:13. There, when the Spirit of Yahweh is said to "grip" David, it is "she grasped" him. And then continues the significant account in 1 Samuel 16:14–23, which displays the fact that the "spirit" of a being is merely an attribute that is spoken of with feminine verb forms. The Hebrew language states, "she withdrew," regarding the removal of God's Spirit from Saul; and also when God sends an evil spirit to terrorize Saul, it says, "she frightened" him.

This usage of the designation of the Spirit of God as a neuter term because it denotes an attribute of God's being is consistently used by the writers of the New Testament. An example is found in Rom 8:16, where Paul says, "the Spirit himself testifies with our spirit that we are God's children." The NIV translators arbitrarily chose to translate the neuter terms as masculine, no doubt pressured by the supposition that the Spirit is a distinct personage within the Trinity and so must be regarded as masculine. This treatment by translators is commonly found in our English versions of the Bible. But it is not true to the Greek text. There, Paul says literally that "the Spirit itself (*auto to pneuma*) testifies to the spirit (*to pneumati*) of us, etc." In both cases of the designations of God's Spirit or our spirits, it is the neuter terminology that is used.

The Holy Spirit is not to be regarded as merely God's supernatural power itself but as the *localized personal presence* of the one true God who then puts forth supernatural power to affect either men or things in creation. This can be seen by the scriptural texts which mention personal attributes such as the "mind" of the Spirit (Rom 8:27), the "speaking" of the Spirit (Acts 8:29; Acts 13:2), the "intercession" of the Spirit (Rom 8:26), and the "grieving" of the Spirit (Isa 63:10; Eph 4:30). The "Presence" of God is always attended with "great strength" (Deut 4:37).

The New Testament authors understood the fact, as Moses did, that the Spirit of God is only the mode of God's localized presence and is the *same phenomenon* as the localized presence of the incarnate God, the Lord Jesus Christ. This is because Yahweh is incarnate in the man Jesus. This is why at times the Spirit of God is either called the "Spirit of Jesus" (Acts 16:7), "the Spirit of Christ" (Rom 8:9; 1 Pet 1:11), or the "the Spirit of Jesus Christ" (Phil 1:19). How Paul describes the Spirit in Galatians 4:6 is very telling. It says, "God sent the Spirit of his Son into our hearts." This is because God's Son is the man Jesus in whom Yahweh is incarnate. And so, God in heaven, by regarding his Son objectively as a distinct person, can speak of his Son's divine presence being dispensed to the believers' hearts. The Greek language in Philippians 1:19, for example, makes it clear that the Spirit is the Spirit *of Jesus Christ* (*tou pneumatos Iesou Christou*). These New Testament designations disprove the doctrine that the Holy Spirit is a distinct member of the "triune" Godhead. The very fact that the Spirit can be *interchangeably regarded* as "of the Father" and also "of the Messiah" shatters the notion of the Spirit as a separate member of a supposed Trinity. But this can be easily understood if the very *unitary essence* of Yahweh is embodied in the Messiah.

The foundational Torah narrative revealed all of the nature of God, and nothing new was disclosed during the era of the Hebrew prophets. The

Spirit of God is the special presence of God. The Spirit is never regarded as a separate person to be worshiped alongside Yahweh. The New Testament is consistent with these facts because *the Holy Spirit is nowhere directly worshiped, praised, thanked, or prayed to* for any blessing given by God the Father or the Lord Jesus Christ. This was the understanding of Moses. This was the Jewish understanding according to the Hebrew Bible. This was the Jewish understanding of Jesus and the apostles. Unless these facts are fully appreciated, and the Jewish sense firmly retained, no one is *prepared* to read the writings of the New Testament accurately whenever the Holy Spirit is mentioned by either Jesus or the apostles.

4

The Hebrew Prophets

IN THE TORAH, MOSES was the premier prophet who taught the covenanted nation of Israel not only the moral and ceremonial will of God but also was instrumental in disclosing the true nature of the only real God whom they should fear and love. The full nature of God, at least that which was necessary for salvation, was revealed during the foundational Torah events, and nothing more was revealed during the subsequent period of the Hebrew prophets or the later New Testament era. The purpose of God's covenant with Israel was to form a people who would experience the glory and the goodness of God in their lives and to love him as the supreme Being in return. Israel was rescued from Egyptian bondage, and then commanded to appreciate God's grace and to give their supreme love in response and glorify him by holiness in the midst of a world who does not know him.

But a necessary requirement for worshiping God correctly is a sufficient knowledge of the nature of his Being so as to adore him according to his glory without distortion and contradiction. No created being can know the infinite God thoroughly. But an apprehension of his essential Being is obviously possible because this much is revealed in the Bible. For examples, if Moses says Yahweh is alone in the created universe and it had derived solely from him, then we can know that there is no other divine being existing. And if Moses says Yahweh is holy, then we can know he does not take secret delight in human vileness. Therefore, our love can rest entirely in the specific apprehension of this God found in the Bible.

In Deuteronomy 18:14–22, Moses informed Israel that Yahweh will raise up further prophetism similar to Moses for direction in their lives as the people of God. This was to satisfy the people's request that a spokesman would speak for God, rather than God himself speaking directly to them, who was terrifying to the congregation (vv 16–17). So, there would then be future Hebrew prophets who would further reveal the will of God to Israel. Sadly, the prophets would also pronounce judgments for disobedience to the national covenant with Yahweh.

This Mosaic announcement was not strictly a messianic prophecy referring to Jesus' role as the final Prophet (Heb 1:1–2). It was a general provision going forward (vv 14, 20–22) given with general principles stating that when a prophet is raised up, he must be obeyed because he will be speaking in the name of God. This directive was basic compared to the significant warning concerning God's "angel" in whom the "Name" of God was "within him," and therefore a weightier warning to revere him (Exod 23:20–22). In Acts 3:17–26, we see evidence how the apostles understood this announcement because they mention how "beginning with Samuel, all the prophets who have spoken have foretold these days" of the Messiah (v 24); this is why the apostles said to the Jews, "you are heirs of the prophets and of the covenant God made with your fathers" (v 25).

It is important to bear in mind that this further prophetism, supernaturally impelled by God's Spirit, became the means by which the *completed* gospel message of grace was prophesied for all the world. The core grace of the covenant with Abraham—by which God will bless all peoples through the descendant of Abraham—stated the *intention* of God. But the further Hebrew prophets anticipated the New Testament gospel by revealing the *specifics* of both the descendant of Abraham and the plan of redemption. Consequently, it is also important to bear in mind that when God had finally *fulfilled* the gospel message by raising up the Messiah Jesus, the Savior's apostles developed and preached their gospel message *strictly* from their only Bible, the Old Testament, written by Moses and the Hebrew prophets. This is the reverent attitude that both the Lord Jesus and the apostles confessed in the New Testament.

Jesus said to his disciples, "Everything must be fulfilled that is written about me in the Law of Moses, the Prophets and the Psalms" (Luke 24:44). Peter preached about the divine intention of the crucifixion of Jesus saying, "But this is how God fulfilled what he had foretold through all the prophets, saying that his Messiah would suffer," and again, "Indeed, beginning with Samuel, all the prophets who have spoken have foretold these days. And you are heirs of the prophets and of the covenant God made with your fathers. He said to Abraham, 'Through your offspring all peoples on earth will be blessed'" (Acts 3:18, 24–25). Paul protested to King Agrippa, "But God has helped me to this very day; so I stand here and testify to small and great alike. I am saying nothing beyond what the prophets and Moses said would happen—that the Messiah would suffer and, as the first to rise from the dead, would bring the message of light to his own people and to the Gentiles" (Acts 26:22–23). Paul also described his biblical ministry, saying, "Paul, a servant of Christ Jesus, called to be an apostle and set apart for the gospel of God—the gospel he promised beforehand through his prophets in the Holy Scriptures regarding his Son, who as to his earthly life was a descendant of David, and who through the Spirit of holiness was appointed the Son of God in power by his resurrection from the dead: Jesus Christ our Lord" (Rom 1:1–4).

The Hebrew prophets and seers that God had raised up after the career of Moses were not employed to add any new understanding of the nature of the Godhead, nor to add any new stipulation to the original Mosaic covenant. Rather, they were sent to warn and rebuke the disobedient nations of Israel and Judah to repent and keep the Mosaic covenant just as it had been given through the ministry of Moses. As stated in the history book, "The Lord warned Israel and Judah through all his prophets and seers: 'Turn from your evil ways. Observe my commands and decrees, in accordance with the entire Law that I commanded your ancestors to obey and that I delivered to you through my servants the prophets'" (2 Kgs 17:13). As Daniel prayed, "All Israel has transgressed your law and turned away, refusing to obey you. Therefore the curses and sworn judgments written in the Law of Moses, the servant of God, have been poured out on us, because we have sinned against you" (Dan 9:11). And at the end of the Old Testament history of Israel and Judah nothing new was demanded from the people except to keep the original Mosaic covenant, as Malachi warned, "Remember the law of my servant Moses, the decrees and laws I gave him at Horeb for all Israel" (Mal 4:4). The people were not to add or take away from it, as Moses warned them, saying, "Do not add to what I command you and do not subtract from it, but keep the commands of the LORD your God that I give you" (Deut 4:2). Therefore, the Hebrew prophets maintained the Torah understanding of the nature and will of God. And the prophets added nothing new to the understanding of the nature of the Godhead of Yahweh, but they did add greater disclosure concerning the coming of the final Messiah, his person, his service, and his salvation.

The test and boundary by which any modern expression of the New Testament gospel can be assessed as being true to divine revelation is how the essential ideas being taught compare to the *plainly revealed ideas* of Moses and the Hebrew prophets. The revelation of the Old Testament as finally authoritative for a right relationship with God was the conviction of even the Hebrew prophets themselves, as warned in Isaiah 8:20: "Consult God's instruction and the testimony of warning. If anyone does not speak according to this word, they have no light of dawn." And the psalmist says, "I have hidden your word in my heart that I might not sin against you" (Ps 119:11). And in Luke 24:25, it was the expressed conviction of the Lord Jesus when he warned his disciples saying, "How foolish you are, and how slow to believe all that the prophets have spoken!" The New Testament gospel message was gathered by the apostles from their Hebrew Bible. Therefore, evangelical Christians should be able to present the gospel message from the Old Testament as well. If they cannot do so, then their understanding of the Old Testament is deficient, or it may be distorted. Christians should be careful *not to say anything beyond what Moses and the prophets said would be known and happen.* If a theological idea is insisted on as divine revelation but which term or concept cannot be *easily displayed* by reasonable and indisputable texts of Old Testament scriptures or cannot be seen to be the expressed conviction of the New Testament church, then it is to be questioned or rejected.

With the Hebrew prophets, we learn, especially from those who wrote their revelation, significant facts concerning the male child of Genesis 3:15 and the descendant of Abraham in Genesis 22:18. We learn nothing additional to the nature or makeup of God's essential Being. But we do learn additional knowledge describing the nature of the prophesied Messiah's coming, his character, his service, through whom God's people will be redeemed and blessed, because God had promised Abraham that "through your offspring all nations on earth will be blessed" (Gen 22:18).

The Old Testament prophets revealed primarily *the man* whom God had chosen, predestined, and anointed to be his pre-eminent servant, his final king, and his final high priest. In other words, though especially the prophet Isaiah intimated the actual incarnation of God in the birth of the male child given for Israel, the prophets ordinarily disclosed facts concerning only the manward aspect of the God-man. In the New Testament, the martyr Stephen described the prophets as "those who predicted the coming of the Righteous One" (Acts 7:52). However, they revealed precious little about *the incarnation of God* within this coming Messiah. Several intimations of the bodily incarnation of Yahweh was all that was mentioned by these prophets in the Old Testament. But it was the apostles and evangelists of the New Testament who were the prophets to confirm and widely proclaim the incarnation of Yahweh bodily in the Lord Jesus Christ. From the Torah we know a few certain facts about the Messiah already, though some of the details are only ascertained from the apostolic affirmations in the New Testament: He would be a male descendant of our fallen humanity, sharing our flesh and blood but not sharing our sinful nature. He would be specifically the descendant of Abraham the Hebrew. All peoples of the earth would be blessed through this descendant of Abraham. The future kingship of the nation, especially the kingdom of the Messiah, would come through the tribe of Judah. The Torah also disclosed, by means of typology, that the Messiah himself would be the final sacrifice slain for atonement for the sins of his people; and that he would perfectly fulfill the priesthood by becoming the means of ever living intercession. These types were confirmed by the New Testament.

From the Torah, we learn about the necessity of the priesthood and blood sacrifice. But then with the subsequent history of Israel, especially during the glorious reign of King David, we learn that God also intended to provide an excellent anointed ruler over Israel, because the people had requested that they would have a king to rule over them like other nations around them rather than have Yahweh rule over them directly. But he will be adopted and dear to God as his son, reigning as his faithful representative over the nation of Israel. Then the writing prophets were eventually employed by the Spirit of God to predict many distinctive facts about the coming, final Anointed One. This book will only consider the prophecies about the Messiah's actual appearing, his actual person, and his service to God.

In the book of Isaiah, we have perhaps the most significant prophecies concerning the nature of the person of the Messiah. But it is also important to notice the understanding of the nature of God that the prophet himself discloses in his ministry. This will in turn strengthen the correct understanding of the nature of the person of the Messiah. In Isaiah 6:1–13, we have the account of the prophet Isaiah's encounter with God and his divine commission. The prophet says, "In the year that King Uzziah died, I saw the Lord, high and exalted, seated on a throne; and the train of his robe filled the temple" (v 1). The Hebrew language is: *va-areh eth-adonay yosheb al-kissa ram vanissa vashulayv mileyim eth-haheykal.* Isaiah calls God "My Lord," whom the seraphim angels call "Yahweh" (v 3). Isaiah somehow *saw* the Lord. He (singular and alone) was seated on a throne, high and exalted. There was only the train of his robe alone that filled the temple. At this time, no one shared the divine throne with Yahweh—not the supposed eternal Son, nor the supposed person of the Holy Spirit. The Messiah had not yet been born, crucified, resurrected, exalted and seated at the right hand of God. Until then, no one shares the divine throne. The trinitarian fiction, which teaches that the Holy Spirit is a separate person within the Godhead who is equally worshiped, is not at all known to Moses, Isaiah, or the Hebrew prophets. The Holy Spirit is never depicted with Yahweh on the throne.

We have seen that Yahweh is known as the "Father," the one-person Creator and Redeemer of Israel (Deut 32:6). Here the prophet Isaiah saw "his Lord," and the angels call the Lord "Yahweh." Isaiah saw only one personal Being, seated on a throne alone. The Lord's robe alone filled his temple. It was his temple alone. When the Lord wanted to send someone to preach to the nation, he alone would send someone, although Yahweh asks the attending angels, just as he had with the creation of humanity in the book of Genesis. Therefore, whenever Isaiah mentions Yahweh in his prophecies, we can know that this name refers to the person of the Father of Israel rather than a complex divine being. Isaiah somehow saw the Lord, but he did not see the Trinity, nor did he see the eternal Son, nor did he see the Holy Spirit sharing the divine throne.

In Isaiah 9:1–7, we have probably the most important passage predicting the incarnation of God. The Galilee region of Israel will be honored by God. It will be honored because of the gracious help of the coming Messiah. The prophet says, "For to us a child is born, to us a son is given, and the government will be on his shoulders. And he will be called Wonderful Counselor, Mighty God, Everlasting Father, Prince of Peace" (v 6). The Hebrew poetry listing the names employs a *chiasmus,* whereby the terms involved exegete each other in a cross pattern. "Wonderful Counselor" refers to "Prince of Peace," and "Mighty God" refers to "Everlasting Father." The first couple seem to have in mind the humanity of the incarnate God because God himself would not be a mere prince or act as a mere counselor, and the second couple certainly regard the Deity of the incarnate God, named as Mighty God and Father of Everlasting. This given son will be known as the "Mighty God," meaning Yahweh, just as he was called the "Mighty God" by the prophet Isaiah (Isa 10:21). The name "Everlasting Father" as it is in the English version is in the Hebrew language as "Father of Everlasting" or "Creator of Time" *(abiad).* It does not mean an "Eternal Father" in the trinitarian sense referring to the supposed first person within the complex Godhead. It should also be noticed that the son given to Israel is not named as the supposed "Eternal Son," as one would think if the Trinity dogma was true. No one in the Hebrew Bible was ever named as God himself. The name format for an ordinary person was always a *reference to* the glory of God, such as "Yah is my strength" in the name Uzziah, or "El is my judge" in the name Daniel. But here the predicted one born will be *regarded as God.*

It is important to appreciate that the predicted one is a *human male child that will be born* as all babies who come into the world. He will be real flesh and blood and having a soul. In Micah 5:2–4, we have another prophecy predicting and confirming the coming of the incarnate God through the birth of a son. We read in verse 3: "Therefore Israel will be abandoned until the time when she who is in labor bears a son." This son will be the "ruler over Israel," whose prediction was "from of old, from ancient times" (v 2), and he will "stand and shepherd his flock in the strength of the LORD, in the majesty of the name of the LORD his God" (v 4). The phrase "of old, from ancient times" means the era of the references found in Genesis 49 and Numbers 24. In a similar sense, Micah himself uses it later in 7:14, 20, referring to the times of Abraham and Moses. This phrase does not mean before time, or the eternal past, which the trinitarians pretend it means to forcibly support the fiction of the "eternal generation" of "God the Son."

Also, what should be appreciated is that the son to be born is the *new* thing. It is well known that Almighty God is eternal as the "Everlasting Father" (rather, as the Creator of time itself). But the new thing is *the introduction of the male child who will be known as God* into both the body of revealed theology and the world of humanity. And with the introduction of this son, there are now *two persons who will be honored as the one Almighty God.* This will commence when the crucified and resurrected son is exalted to the right hand of God on his throne. The people of God can rest in this new thing because it is the determined, passionate plan of God for his glory, as the prophet says in Isaiah 9:7: "The zeal of the LORD Almighty will accomplish this." From now on, there will always be two persons, and only two persons, worshiped as God in both the church and in heaven.

In Isaiah 11:1–9, more of the person and the character of the Messiah's reign is prophesied. He will be a descendant of Jesse, the father of King David. He will be called the "Branch" and will bear fruit. The Spirit of Yahweh will rest on him, enabling him with grace to rule righteously, wisely, and reverently before God. The two important considerations for our study are his real humanity and his real need for the anointing of the Spirit of God for his ministry for the glory of God. He descends from the "stump" of Jesse. Therefore, he will be known as the "son of David." He will not be an angel from heaven, nor will he be from any other nation, nor will he be from any other tribe of Israel. He must be from the nation of Israel, from the tribe of Judah, from the family of Jesse, and from the line of David. Also, his humanity will be real so that he will need the actual enabling of the Spirit of God as would any other mere human being needing the strength of God to do the will of God. He will also "delight in the fear of the LORD" (v 3). But God does not worship God. This is the human who worships Yahweh and serves him faithfully. The Messiah will be Yahweh incarnate, but he will love and fear Yahweh as his God.

In Psalm 2, we have a royal psalm of Israel, anonymously written. It begins with the presumed fact of the hatred of mankind for the rule of God in their lives. But their rebellious attitude is scoffed by God as futile. It declares the decree of Yahweh to have his select king to be enthroned in Zion over Israel and the world. Several theological facts must be noticed from this psalm: The rebellious rulers of the earth are only aware of Yahweh and his anointed king, as it says in verse 2: "The kings of the earth rise up and the rulers band together *against the* LORD *and against his anointed*" (al-yhvh va-al-mashiycho). Hatred is felt for only *two persons*. There is no Trinity existing here. Yahweh is the single-person Deity who is enthroned alone in heaven (v 4). The Hebrew language regards a single person verbally: "He that sits in the heavens," "he laughs," "my Lord," "he holds them in derision" (*yosheb bashamayim yischaq adonay yela-ag-lamo*). The decrees of God, by their very nature, always have a beginning. They announce something new. The king proclaims Yahweh's decree, saying, "You are my son; *today I have become your father*" (v 7). Yahweh invites the anointed king to *ask* him for the nations to be his inheritance (v 8). The nations were not inherently the property of the Messiah when his humanity is considered. They are given to him.

From verse 7, the trinitarians teach the fiction of the *eternal generation* of the supposed second person of the Trinity. It was the brainchild of the early church Christian scholar named Origen in the 200s AD. But the idea is violently derived from this verse, contrary to the traditional Jewish sense of the verse describing God's adoption of the anointed king of Israel as his "son," according to the scriptural sense in 2 Samuel 7:4–17. This idea of eternal generation is so momentous that it would cause a sea-change in divine reality. But it is palpably stupid and desperately gathered from the air. It is a sly form of polytheism. Such a momentous teaching should be disclosed expressly by the Hebrew prophets somewhere, and then explained by the plain-speaking New Testament apostles for even the good of the common, uneducated believer. The idea is never mentioned anywhere. But according to an honest interpretation of this psalm, the only son that Yahweh is aware of in his reality is the king whom he adopts by his decree.

In Zechariah 9:9, we have another prophecy which involves the real humanity of the Messiah. He will come to Zion with the very human-place characteristic of lowliness and he will be riding a donkey, an animal selected for a gentle ruler under God. Yahweh was Israel's first true king (1 Sam 12:12), and subsequent human kings were but representatives of the Majesty of heaven. Earlier in the prophecy of Zechariah, Yahweh encourages Zion to be glad because *He is coming to Zion* to live among her people (Zech 2:10). This will take place when Yahweh is incarnate in the Messiah because then "many nations will be joined with the LORD in that day and will become *my* people" (Zech 2:11). Through these prophecies of Zechariah, we are made to know the precious and breathtaking beauty of God's grace by his willingness to come to live among his redeemed people in the mode of a gentle and humble man of God.

In Psalm 110, we have the foundation text for the astonishing determination of Yahweh, the sole Creator and Ruler over heaven and earth, to *invite* another person to sit on his throne and to assume the rule of the universe, as co-regent of God, by virtue of uniting the Messiah's humanity with himself. In verse 1, we have probably the most important verse quoted about the Messiah in the New Testament: "The LORD says to my lord: 'Sit at my right hand until I make your enemies a footstool for your feet.'" This verse is an important foundation for the argument of this book. Several facts need to be recognized from this psalm: Yahweh speaks as the single-person Deity. Yahweh speaks as being, at first, *alone* on his divine throne. The person being invited to sit at Yahweh's right hand *did not originate from the throne.* That person is being invited to sit at Yahweh's right hand because that position of honor was not his originally.

The person invited is evidently a *man* because he is also appointed by Yahweh to be "a priest forever, in the order of Melchizedek" (v 4). The mediating offices of priest and high priest are only given to men, which is affirmed in Hebrews 5:1, 4: "Every high priest is selected from among the people and is appointed to represent the people in matters related to God, to offer gifts and sacrifices for sins," and, "no one takes this honor on himself, but he receives it when called by God, just as Aaron was." The other person invited is evidently a man because he is *ordered* to sit with Yahweh on his throne, which is not his inherently. The other person invited is evidently a man because he has *enemies* somewhat different from Yahweh's as they are termed "your enemies." And these enemies are described as "kings," "nations," "the dead," "rulers of the whole earth" (vv 5–6). The other person invited is evidently a man because "he will drink from a brook along the way" (v 7). This man is invited by Yahweh to share the divine throne and consequently is regarded by David as his "lord" (v 1). This man is invited by Yahweh to share the divine throne; therefore, *he does not originate from this role.* Again, it should be noticed that in this psalm only *two persons* are regarded for our attention. No Trinity is honored here.

This interpretation regarding this man's *first approach* is confirmed by a similar scenario revealed in Daniel 7:13, which says, "In my vision at night I looked, and there before me was one like a son of man, *coming* with the clouds of heaven. He *approached* the Ancient of Days and *was led into his presence.*" In neither this scenario nor Psalm 110 is there any natural sense that this person originated from the eternal past existing alongside the eternal God. To insist on this idea as a Biblical teaching is to see phantoms and to freely add to scripture. Psalm 110 is historically misread and abused by the trinitarians. The Trinity dogma teaches the fiction of Jesus originating from heaven, temporarily relinquishing his divine throne for the ministry of the cross, and then ascending to heaven to resume sitting at the right hand of God. But the Hebrew prophets never disclosed such an idea anywhere in the Old Testament scriptures, and it is never taught by Christ's apostles anywhere in the New Testament. Such a momentous teaching, constituting a sea-change of divine reality, and supposedly a required belief for salvation, should not be dependent on mere speculation. In fact, this idea was first provoked by the misreading of the prologue to John's Gospel, which will be demonstrated later. But this Psalm 110 is clear: he is a man invited *to begin sharing the throne of God* as well as serve as priest. This needs to be underscored: this man begins to share the divine throne *even as he begins the priesthood.* Both roles were begun by an invitation from Yahweh. It was the new plan of God. It was new to the nation of Israel.

In Daniel 7:9–14, we have an especially important prophecy concerning the Messiah and *the glory that will be given to him by the will of God.* Here, God is called "the Ancient of Days," which is probably a similar concept to Isaiah's "Father of Everlasting" in Isaiah 9:6. This seventh chapter was written in the Aramaic language, which is a related language to Hebrew. Daniel (or the writer of the book) had an uncommon style of phraseology. He often used the word "like," especially when describing his visions. For examples, he will mention seeing a beast or a man as "like a lion" (v 4), or "like a human being" (v 4), or "like a bear" (v 5), or "like a leopard" (v 6). So, when we read in verse 13 about the appearance of the Messiah as "one like a son of man," we can know that it is merely the phrasing that Daniel used to describe visions. There is never anything deeper to perceive when encountering this phrase in other visions, so we can know there is no deeper meaning to this description of the Messiah that we read of in Daniel 7:13. And in verse 14, we read how the Messiah was given the very honor of God as the ruler over all the nations forever.

Important details should be noticed in this passage: God, who is called "the Ancient of Days," is regarded as a single Person who sits on a single throne. The Messiah is called "one like a son of man." We have already seen this phrasing used for all kinds of things which are seen in a vision and which have no hidden meaning. More importantly, the Messiah is called a son of man with the term *enosh,* rather than *adam.* This term for a man connotes his mere humanity and mortality. It does not connote an eternal divine being, as some trinitarians pretend. Myriads of angelic beings "stood before" God and served him, even as "a river of fire was flowing, coming out from before him" (v 10). The term "before" is used by the writer to mean something or someone that serves God as a created thing naturally does.

That creature that serves God is always *before the throne* rather than on it. The simple principle is that whatever is before the throne of God *serves God* and is not God. The writer goes on to say that the Messiah came "on the clouds of heaven," and "approached" the Ancient of Days, and "was led into his presence" (v 13). He was before God just as the angels and the river of fire were before God on his throne. This means that the Messiah was brought near to God to serve him as a mere man would. The Messiah is a real human being.

What is also especially important in this passage is that we see the Messiah must first *approach* God. He did not originate from the eternal presence of God, as the trinitarians pretend. To assert that idea is to add to scripture and breeds confusion. Are we talking about a divine being or a human being? There is no satisfying reason that the trinitarians can provide to explain the omission of such a momentous detail if it were true. The fact of the Messiah's first approach to God is also supported by the other statements. He was seen "coming with the clouds of heaven," and he "was led into his presence." The "clouds of heaven" expression signifies that the event is happening according to the divine plan. It happened because of the will of God to bring this son of man into the presence of God, rather than the man's own attempt. The Messiah was "led into" God's presence, meaning he came from outside the throne room of God. All these expressions point to a first approach. The first approach of this son of man is also supported by what happens to him. Verse 14 says, "He was given authority, glory, and sovereign power; all nations and peoples of every language worshiped him." And this *given* dominion will be an everlasting dominion. However, God himself *already had sovereign dominion over all nations.* God himself *already was worshiped by myriads of angels.* Only God can *give* to someone else the glory of his sovereignty. But this is what he does give to this son of man. Therefore, the Messiah begins, when his humanity is considered, as a mere man and then is given the glory of God's reign. This is the teaching of the New Testament. And we know from Isaiah that a son is given who will be known as the Mighty God. And later in the New Testament we will see that it is *because of the incarnation of God in a certain man* as being the very reason the glory of God can possibly be given to that man. Again, it should be noticed that in this Daniel passage only *two persons* are regarded for our attention. No Trinity is honored here.

The book of Isaiah records five very important songs concerning the predestined Messiah, which are found in chapters 42, 49, 50, 52–53, and 61. These are extremely important prophecies concerning Israel's Messiah because they contain specific details about his calling, his real humanity, his service, and his relationship with God. Earlier in this chapter, we have seen that the Messiah will be God incarnate (Isa 9:6). He will not be a mere man. But all of these songs will only speak of his real humanity and *the role that only his humanity can fulfill.*

The calling and the service of the Messiah as a prophet was unique because he was announced by Yahweh himself before he actually raised him up onto the scene of history. The Servant of Yahweh was announced: "Here is my servant, whom I uphold, my chosen one in whom I delight" (Isa 42:1). And God announced the unique service of the Messiah as no other prophet had done for them. Yahweh says, "Here is my servant" (Isa 42:1). And, correspondingly, the Messiah says, "Listen to me" (Isa 49:1). All other prophets were not announced beforehand to their calling except the role of John the baptizer as the prophet Elijah because he was the forerunner of this Servant of Yahweh (Mal 4:5).

Israel's Messiah was selected from out of all humanity: "My chosen one" (Isa 42:1), similar to the Israelites, the elect people of God. He was *a planned human being* to be born into the Hebrew race at the proper time. However, the Messiah was also chosen to be born *without the sinful nature of fallen humanity,* as we will see affirmed in the New Testament. He was a Hebrew descendant of Abraham, from the tribe of Judah, and from the line of David. The Messiah was in fact predestined before the creation of the world, similar to the predestination of the elect people of God, as the Servant says, "Before I was born the LORD called me; from my mother's womb he has spoken my name" (Isa 49:1; and see Eph 1:4–5).

The especially important detail of the Messiah's *sinless character* is generally intimated throughout the prophets in the Old Testament revelation. But the fact is positively affirmed both by the Lord Jesus himself and the apostles in the New Testament. In the book of Isaiah alone, we have these statements which teach the sinless character of the Messiah: "He will reign on David's throne and over his kingdom, establishing and upholding it with justice and righteousness" (Isa 9:7); "He will not judge by what he sees with his eyes, or decide by what he hears with his ears; but with righteousness he will judge the needy, with justice he will give decisions for the poor of the earth" (Isa 11:3–4); "Righteousness will be his belt and faithfulness the sash around his waist" (Isa 11:5); "In love a throne will be established; in faithfulness a man will sit on it—one from the house of David—one who in judging seeks justice and speeds the cause of righteousness" (Isa 16:5); "In faithfulness he will bring forth justice" (Isa 42:3); "The Sovereign LORD has opened my ears; I have not been rebellious, I have not turned away," and, "He who vindicates me is near. Who then will bring charges against me? Let us face each other! Who is my accuser? Let him confront me! It is the Sovereign LORD who helps me. Who will condemn me?" (Isa 50:5, 8–9); "Though he had done no violence, nor was any deceit in his mouth" (Isa 53:9); "By his knowledge my righteous servant will justify many" (Isa 53:11).

Especially from the book of Isaiah do we learn that the Messiah's ministry was to be mainly a ministry of preaching and teaching about the true kingdom of God, as well as his sacrificial death for his people. Regarding the ministry of the word, we have these statements: "And he will be called Wonderful Counselor" (Isa 9:6); "He will strike the earth with the rod of his mouth; with the breath of his lips he will slay the wicked" (Isa 11:4); "He made my mouth like a sharpened sword" (Isa 49:2); "The Sovereign LORD has given me a well-instructed tongue, to know the word that sustains the weary" (Isa 50:4). The message of the Messiah's preaching is stated succinctly as, "He will bring justice to the nations," and, "In faithfulness he will bring forth justice" (Isa 42:1, 3). This message of "justice" uses the Hebrew word *mishpat*, meaning "judgment"; and it means *the truth about Yahweh's sole Lordship over the universe and his powerful salvation*. And this interpretation is confirmed when the prophet says, "In his teaching the islands will put their hope" (Isa 42:4).

And regarding the ministry of atonement, we have these statements from the great Isaiah chapter 53: "He was despised and rejected by mankind, a man of suffering, and familiar with pain" (v 3); "Surely he took up our pain and bore our suffering" (v 4); "But he was pierced for our transgressions, he was crushed for our iniquities; the punishment that brought us peace was on him, and by his wounds we are healed. We all, like sheep, have gone astray, each of us has turned to our own way; and the LORD has laid on him the iniquity of us all. He was oppressed and afflicted, yet he did not open his mouth; he was led like a lamb to the slaughter, and as a sheep before its shearers is silent, so he did not open his mouth" (vv 5–7); "For he was cut off from the land of the living; for the transgression of my people he was punished" (v 8); "Yet it was the LORD's will to crush him and cause him to suffer, and though the LORD makes his life an offering for sin" (v 10); "By his knowledge my righteous servant will justify many, and he will bear their iniquities" (v 11); "Because he poured out his life unto death, and was numbered with the transgressors. For he bore the sin of many, and made intercession for the transgressors" (v 12).

Another important detail that the Hebrew prophets mention about the Messiah is his *real humanity*. It is impossible, and unthinkable, for God to suffer or die. The Messiah is always depicted as a *man* by the Hebrew prophets and always recognized as such by Christ's apostles. The trinitarians pretend that only the supposed eternal second member of the Godhead ("God the Son") was the person who became incarnate in Jesus and that he was the one who somehow suffered and died on the cross. But when it comes to the crucifixion especially, the trinitarians face the same challenging question: How was the Messiah killed but not God? Believing that "God the Son" had the role as a "sent" member of the Godhead does not eliminate the question. It only breeds more questions. The reality is that the idea of "God the Son" becoming incarnate is a fiction which is nowhere disclosed by the Hebrew prophets. When we pay attention to the Hebrew prophets' very words depicting especially the vicarious suffering of the Messiah, we always read about a man enduring it because *only a man could suffer and die* as a human sacrifice for sinners. We also know the truth, revealed elsewhere, that God will become incarnate in the child given to Israel. But only the man in whom God was incarnate suffered and died while *Yahweh remained united to this man,* somehow in a passive mode, at least up to the point of expiration but always with his living soul. The Messiah's human nature was not altered because of the divine incarnation, nor was he transformed into a superhuman man by mixture or modification due to the two natures being united.

It is an important recognition of both the Hebrew prophets and Christ's apostles that only the manward aspect of the incarnational Being of the Messiah performed his assigned messianic tasks. God himself, in the incarnation, did not perform anything that would be inappropriate for the majestic role of Deity. Rather, it seems that somehow God assumed a *passive role* when united to the man and embodied within him. The son born to Israel is the Branch of Jesse who is the Servant of Yahweh. And the ministry of the Messiah as the Servant of Yahweh will be accomplished with the anointing of the Spirit of Yahweh given to him. God will have become incarnate in the man, from his birth, who is the Anointed One. But it is only the man who performs the service to God, while Yahweh remains fully united to him. In some mysterious manner, Yahweh permanently united his Being to the humanity of the Messiah while the Messiah lived his life of service and suffering, and then death, and then resurrection. The prophets only prophesy experiences that could only pertain to a human being. By the very nature of the events, it is impossible for God to experience them in any real meaningful sense. And all of these depictions are, by the very nature of them, acts of worship in service toward the Deity. In this regard, the trinitarian fiction of the incarnation of the supposed eternal second person experiencing the prophesied events shows up as extremely absurd and blasphemous. The Messiah is depicted as a real man in whom God became incarnate but somehow sustained a passive role for the sake of redemption.

Because of this fact, the Messiah was *empowered for his ministry* by the grant of the Spirit of Yahweh on him. It is an indication of his real, limited, but sinless humanity that he required the enabling of the Spirit just as any man needs to do the will of God. The book of Isaiah makes this fact of the divine enabling of the Messiah clear: "The Spirit of the LORD will rest on him—the Spirit of wisdom and of understanding, the Spirit of counsel and of might, the Spirit of the knowledge and fear of the LORD" (Isa 11:2); "I will put my Spirit on him, and he will bring justice to the nations" (Isa 42:1); "The Spirit of the Sovereign LORD is on me, because the LORD has anointed me to proclaim good news to the poor" (Isa 61:1).

The Servant's *divine calling* was according to the sovereign plan of Yahweh even as any human person is called by God to be his child of grace or to accomplish a certain purpose for the glory of God. It is a fact of scripture that no one takes the honor of a divine calling upon himself but must be given it by the determination of God himself (see Heb 5:4). The Servant's own ministry was first initiated by the predestined purpose of God before the creation of the world even as all the elect people of God were chosen (see Eph 1:4). This divine action "before the creation of the world" is always the New Testament expression of divine predestination, as Peter says of Christ, "He was chosen before the creation of the world, but was revealed in these last times for your sake" (1 Pet 1:20). And whatever needs to be predetermined before the creation of the world was not inherently existing from the eternal past. But in the Old Testament, whenever someone is called by God before the actual birth of that commissioned one, it is to be understood as a vocation predetermined before the creation of the world, as was the calling revealed to the prophet Jeremiah by God saying, "Before I formed you in the womb I knew you (—that is, I loved you), before you were born I set you apart; I appointed you as a prophet to the nations" (Jer 1:5).

The Servant's calling was unique in that he was called "in righteousness"; that is, it was the result of both Yahweh's resolve *to vindicate his real glory through the holiness of his covenant people* and also his resolve *to demonstrate his faithfulness in bringing about his prophesied redemption and restoration of his kingdom on earth.* Yahweh declares, "I, the LORD, have called you in righteousness" (Isa 42:6). No other Hebrew prophet was raised to successfully affect these things despite their faithful ministries. No other prophet was given as "a covenant for the people."

The Servant's calling was unique in that *his personality was divinely fashioned* from birth and throughout his natural development to be the sinless and devoted Messiah that was necessary for the accomplishment of the promised redemption. This was necessary because in this one man Yahweh would definitively display his splendor—his holiness and goodness—by rendering him to be the perfect Israelite who completely fulfills the righteousness of the Mosaic covenant. Yahweh announces his complete pleasure in his chosen servant, saying, "My chosen one in whom I delight" (Isa 42:1); and the Servant testifies, "He said to me, 'You are my servant,

Israel, in whom I will display my splendor'" (Isa 49:3); and Yahweh declares, "I will take hold of your hand. I will keep you and will make you to be a covenant for the people" (Isa 42:6); and again the Servant discloses, "He made my mouth like a sharpened sword, in the shadow of his hand he hid me; he made me into a polished arrow and concealed me in his quiver" (Isa 49:2); and again the Servant says succinctly, "And now the LORD says—he who formed me in the womb to be his servant to bring Jacob back to him and gather Israel to himself, for I am honored in the eyes of the LORD and my God has been my strength" (Isa 49:5); and again the Servant testifies, "The Sovereign LORD has given me a well-instructed tongue, to know the word that sustains the weary. He wakens me morning by morning, wakens my ear to listen like one being instructed" (Isa 50:4).

The Servant needed to be *supernaturally enabled and sustained* in his role as the righteous, faithful, humble Messiah by the divine hand taking hold of him, fashioning him, and upholding him, as Yahweh says, "Here is my servant, whom I uphold," and "I, the LORD, have called you in righteousness; I will take hold of your hand. I will keep you and will make you to be a covenant for the people and a light for the Gentiles, to open eyes that are blind, to free captives from prison and to release from the dungeon those who sit in darkness" (Isa 42:1, 6–7); "In the time of my favor I will answer you, and in the day of salvation I will help you; I will keep you and will make you to be a covenant for the people, etc." (Isa 49:8). Yahweh's divine help was the Servant's confidence, as he says, "Because the Sovereign LORD helps me, I will not be disgraced. Therefore have I set my face like flint, and I know I will not be put to shame," and, "It is the Sovereign LORD who helps me. Who will condemn me?" (Isa 50:7, 9); and again, "The Spirit of the Sovereign LORD is on me, because the LORD has anointed me to proclaim good news to the poor. He has sent me to bind up the brokenhearted, to proclaim freedom for the captives and release from darkness for the prisoners, to proclaim the year of the LORD's favor" (Isa 61:1–2).

The Servant needed to be *disciplined with instruction* just as any human disciple would need, as he says, "The Sovereign LORD has given me a well-instructed tongue, to know the word that sustains the weary. He wakens me morning by morning, wakens my ear to listen like one being instructed. The Sovereign LORD has opened my ears; I have not been rebellious, I have not turned away" (Isa 50:4–5); "He made my mouth like a sharpened sword, in the shadow of his hand he hid me; he made me into a polished arrow and concealed me in his quiver" (Isa 49:2).

The Servant needed to *obey the will of God* in order to fulfill his calling just as any man of God needs to, as he says, "The Sovereign LORD has opened my ears; I have not been rebellious, I have not turned away" (Isa

50:5). The Servant's commission involved the willing sacrifice of his physical body as an offering for sin for the sake of atonement, as the psalmist says, "Sacrifice and offering you did not desire—but my ears you have opened—burnt offerings and sin offerings you did not require. Then I said, 'Here I am, I have come—it is written about me in the scroll'" (Ps 40:6–7). The Servant's self-sacrifice was clearly prophesied in the book of Isaiah: "But he was pierced for our transgressions, he was crushed for our iniquities; the punishment that brought us peace was on him, and by his wounds we are healed," and, "Yet it was the LORD's will to crush him and cause him to suffer, and though the LORD makes his life an offering for sin, he will see his offspring and prolong his days, and the will of the LORD will prosper in his hand" (Isa 53:5, 10).

The Servant *worshiped only Yahweh, the Father of Israel.* The Servant loved, feared, and obeyed only the one-person sovereign Deity who was Yahweh. He had no regard for the Spirit of God as a separate personage alongside Yahweh. The Spirit was the mode of Yahweh's personal, special presence. The Holy Spirit was, as the Messiah says, "the Spirit of the Sovereign LORD" upon him, enabling him for his service (Isa 61:1). Conversely, Yahweh acknowledged that the Messiah served only himself as being the sole personal Deity who had absolute authority over his affairs, as Yahweh says, "Here is my servant, whom I uphold, my chosen one in whom I delight" (Isa 42:1). The Hebrew language says, in my translation, "In him, my choice one, my soul delights" (*bo bachiry ratsthah naphshy*). Yahweh's soul (which is his Spirit) alone delights in the Messiah. The Spirit is not another person who (the trinitarians would think) would delight in him also. The Servant testifies about his relationship of worship with Yahweh alone: "*He* said to me, 'You are *my* servant, Israel, in whom *I* will display *my* splendor,'" and, "*He* who formed me in the womb to be *his* servant . . . *for I am honored in the eyes of the LORD*" (Isa 49:3, 5). The Messiah says he is honored in the eyes of Yahweh alone. He does not mention being honored in the eyes of the Spirit as though he were a separate person alongside the Father. But the Trinity fiction—due to misreading the passage in the Gospel of John, which mentions that the Spirit "will not speak on his own . . . he will glorify me" (see John 16:13–15)—believes there is evidence that the Spirit will honor the Messiah as a separate personage alongside the Father. But this notion flies in the face of the disclosure of the prophet. Yahweh testifies that the promised ruler will be raised up for his service alone, saying, "But you, Bethlehem Ephrathah, though you are small among the clans of Judah, out of you will come *for me* one who will be ruler over Israel" (Mic 5:2). Yahweh describes his called shepherd, saying, "Awake, sword, against *my* shepherd, against the man who is close *to me*" (Zech 13:7).

The Servant *behaved as a real human being*. The Messiah knew himself to be a man who served the God of Israel. Though the Hebrew prophets certainly intimated the incarnation of God in the birth of the son given to Israel, the Messiah nowhere regarded himself as being in the *active role* of Deity during the fulfillment of his calling. He did not live and move among men as a divine being. He was always regarded as a man in the prophecies concerning his service to God: "Before I was born the LORD called me; from my mother's womb he has spoken my name" (Isa 49:1); "I offered my back to those who beat me, my cheeks to those who pulled out my beard; I did not hide my face from mocking and spitting" (Isa 50:6); "He was despised and rejected by mankind, a *man* of suffering, and familiar with pain" (Isa 53:3); "Awake, sword, against my shepherd, against the *man* who is close to me" (Zech 13:7).

We have already seen the prophecies announcing the birth of the Messiah as a male child. We also have these scriptural statements involving his humanity: "Yet you brought me out of the womb; you made me trust in you, even at my mother's breast. From birth I was cast on you; from my mother's womb you have been my God" (Ps 22:9–10); "I am poured out like water, and all my bones are out of joint. My heart has turned to wax; it has melted within me. My mouth is dried up like a potsherd, and my tongue sticks to the roof of my mouth; you lay me in the dust of death. Dogs surround me, a pack of villains encircles me; they pierce my hands and my feet. All my bones are on display; people stare and gloat over me. They divide my clothes among them and cast lots for my garment" (Ps 22:14–18).

It is worth noticing that the Hebrew prophet Ezekiel also demonstrates his understanding of the concept of *spirit* when he records the vision of the "four living creatures" in the first chapter of his book. He says of the movements of the wheels that, "because the spirit of the living creatures was in the wheels" that the wheels moved accordingly (Ezek 1:21). Now, Ezekiel does not mean to imply that the spirits of the four living creatures were to be regarded as separate personages from the four living creatures themselves but only that their immaterial souls somehow animated the wheels. To read this passage with a trinitarian hallucination is to do violence to the natural reading of the account.

5

Jesus the Messiah

WHAT DID JESUS THE Messiah know and believe? What were the religious convictions of Jesus the Jewish man? These questions being answered correctly will be the safest and surest method for learning the true theology of the New Testament church. And as with the Old Testament revelation, we should never add to, or subtract from, the express statements of the Lord Jesus regarding any aspect of the reality of the kingdom of God. By carefully observing what Jesus believed and taught his disciples and how he worshiped with them as the perfect Israelite will reveal to the church what is the *true content* and description of biblical doctrine, and will safeguard biblical theology from the distortions that so often defile it.

It is extremely important to bear in mind that the Messiah was a Hebrew man called by God to be the perfect, sinless Israelite worshiper of Yahweh according to the Mosaic covenant, through whom God would display his splendor and vindicate his glorious name from the reproach of the treachery of his rebellious covenant nation, Israel and then Judah. Consequently, we can discern the content of theological truth by observing what Jesus believed and preached and taught his disciples, and how he understood the Godhead. Jesus is to be regarded, as the Bible does, as a real human being who lived as a real human man does. He is everywhere depicted as a godly Jewish worshiper of the Majesty of heaven rather than as a superhuman being who cannot be touched with the challenges and limitations of earthly existence. He lived and behaved as a man—not as God—until his exaltation to the right hand of the Majesty in heaven.

We have learned that the Hebrew prophets certainly revealed that the Messiah would be the promised Hebrew son given to Israel in whom Yahweh would become incarnate bodily forever. Therefore, the Messiah is both fully God and fully man, somehow united into one person. Two natures were united in this one person, but two real and distinct natures. The divine nature of the one-person God, Yahweh, and the human nature of the man Jesus. I can say this confidently because I observe carefully what the prophet Isaiah said: Yahweh promised that a son would be given to Israel. I read that the one-person God, the Father, will give a promised human son, and that child will be regarded as the Mighty God (Isa 9:6).

Jesus, the prophesied Messiah, when he matured as a man, adopted the lifestyle of a traditional Jewish rabbi who gathered disciples around him to be both redeemed and discipled as devout people of Yahweh, the Father of Israel. Jesus taught his disciples that he came not to abolish the Mosaic covenant but even to fulfill the whole Torah. Therefore, he taught it accurately, and restored its true interpretation despite the distortions and accretions of the unregenerate teachers of the law of Moses (the scribes and the Pharisees and the Sadducees) found in Israel at the time. Jesus also taught his disciples how to pray.

Jesus was a *devout and loving worshiper of Yahweh, the Father of Israel.* Jesus *worshiped only the Father* along with the godly people of Israel and his close disciples. Jesus knew that *the angels of heaven worship and serve the Father alone.* Jesus nowhere shows an awareness of a Trinity, or a complex Godhead. Jesus nowhere honors the Holy Spirit as a separate personage alongside the Father.

These following selected New Testament verses, which contain the express statements of Jesus, demonstrate that the Messiah worshiped the Father alone and encouraged his disciples to worship the Father alone: "Jesus said to him, 'Away from me, Satan! For it is written: Worship the Lord your God, and *serve him only*'" (Matt 4:10); "This, then, is how you should pray: 'Our Father in heaven, hallowed be *your name, your kingdom come, your will be done,* on earth as it is in heaven'" (Matt 6:9–10); "Not everyone who says to me, 'Lord, Lord,' will enter the kingdom of heaven, but only the one who *does the will of my Father* who is in heaven'" (Matt 7:21); "All things have been committed to me *by my Father.* No one knows the Son *except the Father, and no one knows the Father* except the Son and those to whom the Son chooses *to reveal him*" (Matt 11:27; and see Luke 10:22; John 6:46; John 10:15); "Pointing to his disciples, he said, 'Here are my mother and my brothers. For whoever *does the will of my Father in heaven* is my brother and sister and mother'" (Matt 12:49); "For the Son of Man is going to come *in his Father's glory with his angels*" (Matt 16:27); "See that you do not despise one of these little ones. For I tell you that their angels in heaven always see *the face of my Father in heaven*" (Matt 18:10); "Jesus replied: *'Love the Lord your God* (referring to Yahweh the Father of Israel) *with all your heart and with all your soul and with all your mind*'" (Matt 22:37); "And do not call anyone on earth 'father,' for you have one Father, and *he is in heaven*" (Matt 23:9); "But about that day or hour no one knows, not even the angels in heaven, nor the Son, but *only the Father*" (Matt 24:36; and see Mark 13:32); "At that time Jesus said, *'I praise you, Father, Lord of heaven and earth,* because you have hidden these things from the wise and learned, and revealed them to little children'" (Matt 11:25; and see Luke 10:21); "I am going to send you what *my Father has promised*" (Luke 24:49); "I tell you, I will not drink from this fruit of the vine from now on until that day when I drink it new with you *in my Father's kingdom*" (Matt 26:29); " 'Woman,' Jesus replied, 'believe me, a time is coming when you will *worship the Father* neither on this mountain nor in Jerusalem. You Samaritans worship what you do not know; we worship what we do know, for salvation is from the Jews. Yet a time is coming and has now come when the true worshipers will *worship the Father* in the Spirit and in truth, for they are *the kind of worshipers the Father seeks.* God is spirit, and *his worshipers* must worship in the Spirit and in truth'" (John 4:21–24); "That all may honor the Son *just as they honor the Father.* Whoever does not honor the Son *does not honor the Father, who sent him*" (John 5:23); " 'I am not possessed by a demon,' said Jesus, *'but I honor my Father* and you dishonor me'" (John 8:49); "So they took away the stone. Then Jesus looked up and said, *'Father, I thank you that you have heard me'*" (John 11:41); "*I have brought you glory on earth* by finishing the work you gave me to do. *And now, Father, glorify me in your presence* with the glory I had *with you* before the world began" (John 17:4–5); "Jesus said, 'Do not hold on to me, for I have not yet *ascended to the Father.* Go instead to my brothers and tell them, 'I am ascending *to my Father and your Father,* to my God and your God'" (John 20:17).

These following selected New Testament verses confirm, both by the apostolic witness and Jesus himself, that the Messiah served and worshiped God as a godly Jew, according to the manward aspect of his God-man person, and only the Father: "Then the end will come, *when he hands over the kingdom to God the Father* after he has destroyed all dominion, authority and power" (1 Cor 15:24); "And being found in appearance as a man, he humbled himself by becoming obedient to death—even death on a cross! . . . *to the glory of God the Father*" (Phil 2:8, 11); "He says, *'I will declare your name* to my brothers and sisters; in the assembly *I will sing your praises.*' And again, *'I will put my trust in him'*" (Heb 2:12–13); "For this reason he had to be made like them, fully human in every way, in order that he might become a merciful and faithful high priest *in service to God,* and that he might make atonement for the sins of the people" (Heb 2:17); "During the days of Jesus' life on earth, *he offered up prayers and petitions* with fervent cries and tears to the one who could save him from death, and he was heard because of *his reverent submission.* Son though he was, *he learned obedience from what he suffered* (Heb 5:7–8); "He received honor and glory *from God the Father* when the voice came to him from the Majestic Glory, saying, 'This is my Son, whom I love; *with him I am well pleased'*" (2 Pet 1:17); "And has made us to be a kingdom and priests *to serve his God and Father*" (Rev 1:6); "The one who is victorious will, like them, be dressed in white. I will never blot out the name of that person from the book of life, but will acknowledge that name *before my Father* and his angels" (Rev 3:5); "To the one who is victorious, I will give the right to sit with me on my throne, just as I was victorious and sat down *with my Father on his throne*" (Rev 3:21); "Then I looked, and there before me was the Lamb, standing on Mount Zion, and with him 144,000 who had his name and *his Father's name* written on their foreheads" (Rev 14:1).

The Messiah Jesus, as a godly rabbi, commanded and encouraged his disciples to worship, reverence, glorify, and pray to, only the Father, the Lord of heaven and earth, as these selected verses demonstrate: "In the same way, let your light shine before others, that they may see your good deeds and *glorify your Father in heaven*" (Matt 5:16); "But I tell you, love your enemies and pray for those who persecute you, *that you may be children of your Father in heaven.* He causes his sun to rise on the evil and the good, and sends rain on the righteous and the unrighteous" (Matt 5:44–45); "Be perfect, therefore, *as your heavenly Father is perfect*" (Matt 5:48); "So that your giving may be in secret. *Then your Father, who sees what is done in secret, will reward you*" (Matt 6:4); "But when you pray, go into your room, close the door and *pray to your Father, who is unseen. Then your Father, who sees what is done in secret, will reward you*" (Matt 6:6); "For if you forgive other people when they sin against you, *your heavenly Father will also forgive you.* But if you do not forgive others their sins, *your Father will not forgive your sins*" (Matt 6:14–15); "For the pagans run after all these things, and *your heavenly Father knows that you need them. But seek first his kingdom and his righteousness,* and all these things will be given to you as well" (Matt 6:32–33); "If you, then, though you are evil, know how to give good gifts to your children, how much more will *your Father in heaven give good gifts to those who ask him*" (Matt 7:11); "Not everyone who says to me, 'Lord, Lord,' will enter the kingdom of heaven, but only *the one who does the will of my Father who is in heaven*" (Matt 7:21); "But when they arrest you, do not worry about what to say or how to say it. At that time you will be given what to say, for it will not be you speaking, *but the Spirit of your Father speaking through you*" (Matt 10:19–20); "Whoever acknowledges me before others, *I will also acknowledge before my Father in heaven.* But whoever disowns me before others, *I will disown before my Father in heaven*" (Matt 10:32–33); "At that time Jesus said, '*I praise you, Father, Lord of heaven and earth,* because you have hidden these things from the wise and learned, and revealed them to little children" (Matt 11:25); "Pointing to his disciples, he said, 'Here are my mother and my brothers. For *whoever does the will of my Father in heaven is my brother and sister and mother*'" (Matt 12:49–50); "Then *the righteous will shine like the sun in the kingdom of their Father*" (Matt 13:43); "For the Son of Man is *going to come in his Father's glory with his angels, and then he will reward each person according to what they have done*" (Matt 16:27); "See that you do not despise one of these little ones. For I tell you that *their angels in heaven always see the face of my Father in heaven*" (Matt 18:10); "And do not call anyone on earth 'father,' *for you have one Father, and he is in heaven*" (Matt 23:9); "This is my blood of the covenant, which is poured out for many for the forgiveness of sins. I tell you, I will not drink from this fruit of the vine from now on *until that day when I drink it new with you in my Father's kingdom*" (Matt 26:28–29).

In Matthew 6:9–13 (and see Luke 11:2–4), where Jesus teaches how his disciples should pray, he necessarily involves the correct understanding of God's nature. These passages demonstrate the beliefs of the Messiah and how a godly disciple should believe. They show that, consistent with the revelation of the Torah of Moses and the religious convictions of the Hebrew prophets, Yahweh is a single person Deity who is the Creator and Redeemer of Israel, who is called the "Father." Yahweh is also, in a *unique sense,* the Father of the Messiah. Therefore, only the Father is addressed as the Deity to be revered and worshiped and prayed to for such benefits as needs provided, protection, and forgiveness: "Our Father in heaven, hallowed be your name, your kingdom come, your will be done, on earth as it is in heaven. Give us today our daily bread. And forgive us our debts, as we also have forgiven our debtors. And lead us not into temptation, but deliver us from the evil one." *Only the Father is addressed. Only the Father's name is to be hallowed. Only the Father's kingdom and will is to be prayed for and done.*

Before the exaltation of the Lord Jesus, there is only one name to be revered. There is no concern for the complex name of the three members of the supposed Trinity according to the suspicious baptismal formula probably inserted into the Great Commission passage (Matt 28:19). No Trinity is acknowledged here. The Holy Spirit is omitted here, and the Messiah never prays to the Spirit as a supposed separate personage to be worshiped alongside the Father. If there was a real Trinity, the Messiah was unfaithful to God and has misled his disciples by neglecting the disclosure of the complex Godhead and the necessity to believe in the Trinity to be God's real disciples according to the trinitarian theologians. And this, in turn, forces the trinitarians to practice self-deceit in thinking and encouraging the dogma that Jesus actually knew he was a member of the triune God when he taught his disciples to worship and pray to only the Father, which, in turn, effectively makes Jesus a dishonest rabbi. The element of deceit is always present somewhere in the dogma of the Trinity.

In Matthew 11:25–27 (and see Luke 10:21–22), where Jesus praises God, he necessarily involves the correct understanding of God's nature. In this passage, the Messiah praises only the Father, and acknowledges him to be *the sole Lord of heaven and earth,* which is consistent with the revelation of the Torah of Moses and the religious convictions of the Hebrew prophets. Here, Jesus first asserts his divinely given authority and the prerogative to reveal the true God that comes *solely from the Father,* when he says, "All things have been committed to me by my Father" (v 27). And then he says what is extremely important for our study—which no trinitarian pays attention to: Jesus asserts that *only the Father and he share a divinely reciprocal intimate relationship* when he says, "No one knows the Son except the Father, and no one knows the Father except the Son" (v 27). The Holy Spirit is omitted here. If the Spirit was a member of the supposed Trinity, it would be impossible to omit him as knowing the Son as well as the Father does. But here, even Jesus does not know the Spirit as he knows the Father. Again, if the Spirit was a member of the supposed Trinity, it would be impossible to disregard the Spirit's knowledge of either the Father or the Son. If there is a Trinity, the Spirit is shamefully omitted from this divinely reciprocal intimate relationship, which the Father and the Messiah do share. There is no satisfying explanation that the trinitarians can give for this omission.

In John 16:32, we read, "A time is coming and in fact has come when you will be scattered, each to your own home. You will leave me all alone. Yet I am not alone, for *my Father is with me.*" The Messiah alludes to the prophecy of Zechariah, which will unfold by the disciples abandoning Jesus and being scattered to their own homes. But though Jesus will be left alone, he will not be alone. Because he is God's Messiah, he necessarily enjoys a real, intimate, and loving relationship with his God. Therefore, Jesus asserts that though they will leave him to be alone in his mission, he will not really be alone because his heavenly Father is always with him in a loving bond. This close relationship with God happens *to involve only the Father.* No Trinity is acknowledged here. The Spirit is shamefully omitted, and the trinitarians cannot provide a satisfying explanation as to why.

In Matthew 22:41–46 (and see Mark 12:35–37 and Luke 20:41–44), the Messiah challenges the Pharisees, asking them to explain whose son is the Lord of David. The quoted Psalm 110 makes it clear that David, under divine inspiration, says that this amazing divine invitation of sharing the divine throne with a certain man *happened to his Lord*. It was well known from other prophecies that the Messiah in question was certainly to be a son of David. And there was to be only one final Messiah. Therefore, whatever was decreed for the Messiah must be for the one same person. If the Messiah is a son of David, then David's son is also invited to share the divine throne too. But Jesus asks the Pharisees, whose son is he? That is, how can a descendant of David become the Lord of David, which is unnatural? David would naturally be the Lord over any descendant. But the Pharisees could not answer this question to explain this inevitable divine decree.

This encounter proves the falsehood of the Trinity myth. Both the question posed by Jesus and the inability of the Pharisees to answer this specific question *demonstrate that there was no Jewish theological conviction of a Trinity derived from the Old Testament revelation.* If there was a knowledge of the Trinity, including a knowledge of an "eternal Son of God," then the Pharisees would have been able to answer this question by replying that the "eternal Son of God" becomes incarnate in the son of David, as the Trinity dogma asserts. More than this, Jesus would not have asked this specific question if it was common knowledge that God has an "eternal Son" existing from the eternal past alongside him. Of course, the Trinity myth seems silly if Yahweh must invite his "eternal Son" to share the Father's throne at all! However, according to both Jesus and the Pharisees, the person invited to share the divine throne is strictly a son of David, a human being.

We have seen how rabbi Jesus taught his disciples to pray, and therefore to worship only the Father. In Luke 22:39–44, the Messiah prays during deep anguish in the place called Gethsemane, pleading to avoid the agony of the cross. But the Messiah humbly defers to the will of God for finishing the work of redemption. When Jesus prays, he again discloses the nature of the true God. He prays *only to the Father* and uses language which demonstrates the single personage of God, including *his single will.* He prays, "Father, if you are willing, take this cup from me; yet not my will, but yours be done" (v 42). The manward aspect of the God-man Jesus necessarily involves his own will, which makes up his single personage. His human person naturally dreads the agony of the cross. Jesus does not know about a Trinity. And though the prophet Isaiah says the Messiah was anointed with the Spirit of Yahweh to perform his ministry, Jesus does not ask the Spirit separately to help him.

The Messiah *knew that he was God incarnate.* He was aware that he was the predestined son given to Israel who would be known as the "Mighty God" and the "Father of everlasting," as Isaiah prophesied. Jesus certainly knew that he was the embodiment of the Almighty God and therefore, *by virtue of this union of the two natures in his one person,* he was aware that he was "equal to God" (John 10:33; Phil 2:5–6) and was the perfect earthly representative of both the personal presence and the moral character of God and the exact performer of his will (John 10:30; John 14:9–11). This consciousness of his personal equality with God was expressed unequivocally to the unbelieving Jews: "'Very truly I tell you,' Jesus answered, 'before Abraham was born, I am!'" (John 8:58); "I and the Father are one" (John 10:30); "If you really know me, you will know my Father as well. From now on, you do know him and have seen him" (John 14:7).

Trinitarians are embarrassed and struggle to make sense of the famous passages which say that the day or hour especially of the return of the Messiah is not known to him, the God-man. The living God is necessarily omniscient and would know the time of the end of the present age. But in Matthew 24:36, Jesus declares that day or hour is unknown to even himself, saying, "But about that day or hour no one knows, not even the angels in heaven, nor the Son, but only the Father." Jesus delimits the knowledge of the time of the end of the age *to the Father alone.* The Greek language is indisputable: "only the father" (*ei me ho pater monos*). Here, the Messiah honors no Trinity. The Spirit is shamefully omitted. When Jesus lists the possible beings who would know the future, he mentions the angels in heaven who are in the presence of God but does not mention the Holy Spirit who is supposedly a member of the Trinity, supposedly being in council with the Father.

The reason Jesus, "the Son," denied having specific knowledge of the future end times is because *he was living in the role of a man who served God* rather than the role of God himself. Even though he knew he was the prophesied embodiment of Almighty God, his *equality with God was emptied, or suppressed, for the sake of his ministry for the sake of redemption.* Jesus "made himself nothing by taking the very nature (or role) of a servant, being made in human likeness" (Phil 2:6–8). Consequently, and evidently, *his personal consciousness was somehow delimited to the manward aspect of the God-man.* In other words, though Jesus knew that he was Yahweh incarnate bodily and that therefore his human person was equal to God in heaven, his personal consciousness was only the consciousness of his human person called to be an inspired prophet while he served God in heaven. Jesus did not live out his earthly life with the full inherent omniscience of God any more than he lived with the full inherent supernatural power of God.

Jesus disclosed that even the miracles he performed were done by the supernatural power of God in heaven, as he says about exorcism: "But if I drive out demons *by the finger of God,* then the kingdom of God has come upon you" (Luke 11:20), and as this awareness is seen by his gratitude to the Father in heaven, "So they took away the stone. Then Jesus looked up and said, "Father, I thank you that *you have heard me*" (John 11:41). Yahweh was somehow united to the person of Jesus bodily but remained in a *passive mode* during the Messiah's service on earth, at least until his resurrection and exaltation to the right hand of the throne of God. "The Son" is the Jewish man, the descendant of David. He is not the fictional "eternal Son," being co-equal and co-eternal with the other members of the supposed Trinity, and who would naturally know all future matters.

In Matthew 4:1–11, there is evidence that the Messiah regarded the scriptural title of "the Son of God" in the very same way as Satan understood it. Satan correctly and only understood the title to mean that Jesus, *as bearing the title of the Son of God, is a man* rather than an eternal divine being co-equal and co-eternal with the other members of the supposed Trinity. When the devil attempted to cause doubt about Jesus' calling and corrupt the service of the Messiah after his forty days and nights of fasting in the wilderness, the devil enticed Jesus with *situations that would only appeal to humans,* and these irreverent situations are *condemned by the revealed will of God respecting only humans.* More than this, the devil is not so stupid and theologically perverse as to think he could entice God himself to consider these enticements, or that they would even be inappropriate for God to have or experience. For examples, *if God willed,* he could make bread. *If God willed,* he could command his angels to bear him up after falling somehow.

But the fact is, these temptations would only appeal to, and be irreverent for, the *servants* of God only. This is evidenced by the Messiah's scriptural rebukes to the devil. These scriptural references are directed originally toward the people of God as his servants. They never have an application toward God himself. In the passage, Jesus answered the devil, saying, *man* shall not live by bread alone (v 4); and the people of God are commanded not to put the Lord *their God* to the test (v 7); and the people of God are to *worship and serve him only* (v 10). God is worshiped; he does not worship himself as a servant would. God owns all the world and so cannot be enticed with the splendor of the kingdoms of the world. Therefore, the title of "the Son of God," according to both the Messiah and the devil means the especially loved and anointed man of God. It does not mean an "eternal son of God." When the trinitarians insist it means the "eternal son of God," they play games with the scriptures; and they make God, even the supposed triune God, look ridiculous. When it is convenient, they say it means the "eternal son of God." And when it is convenient, they say it means the anointed man Jesus.

In Matthew 26:27–30, where the Messiah discusses the blood of the covenant and an aspect of the future age, he mentions that he will not drink wine ever again until he drinks it new with his disciples in the presence of God, saying, "I tell you, I will not drink from this fruit of the vine from now on until that day when I drink it new with you *in my Father's kingdom*" (v 29). The Messiah regards the kingdom of God as belonging only to the Father. No Trinity is honored here, and the Spirit is shamefully omitted. The Messiah's redemption produces a special union. This special unity of love and fellowship is delimited to the Father, the Messiah, and the disciples (see John 17:20–23).

The passage in Mark 14:32–36, where the Messiah prays in anguish to be possibly excused from the impending agony of the cross, demonstrates his personal consciousness of the manward aspect of the God-man: " 'Abba, Father,' he said, 'everything is possible for you. Take this cup from me. Yet not what I will, but what you will'" (v 36). Jesus prays only to the Father. No Trinity is honored here, and the Spirit is shamefully omitted. Jesus is conscious of his own personal will (as the man in whom God is incarnate), *submitting his will to the Father's will.* The two wills mentioned here demonstrate that we are observing the *two real and different natures of human and divine,* rather than the fictional distinction between two supposed members of the Trinity, because then two wills would prove two deities.

The Messiah Jesus *regarded the Holy Spirit precisely as Moses did,* as being the mode of the special presence of God. Yahweh had said that he was with Israel by his "Presence": "Because he loved your ancestors and chose their descendants after them, he brought you out of Egypt by his Presence and his great strength" (Deut 4:37); "Then his people recalled the days of old, the days of Moses and his people—where is he who brought them through the sea, with the shepherd of his flock? Where is he who set his Holy Spirit among them" (Isa 63:11). It is extremely important to realize the fact that Jesus regarded the Holy Spirit of God as a faithful Jewish adherent of the Torah of Moses and the Hebrew prophets' revelation.

The trinitarians exercise the wretched hermeneutic of circular reasoning because when they first misread the prologue of John's Gospel, thinking there is an "eternal Logos" with God, then there has to be assigned an equally distinct personage to the Holy Spirit, being read-into even in the Old Testament. But Jesus was influenced by the correct antecedent theology of the Old Testament revelation: Moses himself knew of the ministry of the Holy Spirit but nowhere regarded or taught that the Holy Spirit was a distinct member of the supposed Trinity, and nowhere taught Israel to worship such a complex Godhead. The Hebrew prophets plainly regarded the Spirit of God as his presence.

When Jesus discusses the gift of the Holy Spirit as a second Advocate (or the Paraclete) and regards it as an attribute of God's being (such as his "soul,"), he refers to the Spirit with the Greek neuter term "it" (*auto*) in John 14:17. And when the man, Jesus, discusses the Spirit as the presence of God, he refers to "him" (*auton*) in John 16:7. And Jesus describes the Spirit as the "Spirit of truth," meaning the only Spirit that the readers of the Old Testament scriptures would know of. And the man, Jesus, describes the Spirit as that which "goes out from the Father" in John 15:26. The Greek term (*ekporeuetai*) means to "proceed from" or "emerge from," such as a small river proceeds from a larger river. The idea is simply an *extension* of the Father's being, not a different being altogether. This description is different from the idea of being "sent" as Jesus the Messiah was.

The apostle Paul speaks similarly in 1 Corinthians 12, where he discusses Spiritual gifts given to the church. In verses 4–6, Paul says, "There are different kinds of gifts, but the same Spirit distributes them. There are different kinds of service, but the same Lord. There are different kinds of working, but in all of them and in everyone it is the same God at work." Paul uses the Greek neuter pronoun "it" for the Spirit when he regards the Spirit as an attribute of God, saying, *to de auto pneuma.* But he uses the masculine gender pronouns when he refers to both the Lord Jesus and God the Father. He says the service of the different gifts are toward the one same Lord Jesus, saying, *ho autos kurios.* Again, Paul uses the masculine gender pronoun when he refers to God the Father as the very one who works his energy in all of these different manifestations of Spiritual gifts, saying, *ho de autos theos, ho energon, etc.* Notice that Paul had said that the Spirit distributed the gifts, and the gifts were in service to the Lord Jesus, but that the working of the gifts were by the energy of the same God. When there is the immediate distribution of gifts into the members of the church, it is through the means of the Holy Spirit—the mode of the special presence of God—but the credit of the operation is given to the one same Father in heaven. Why did Paul not use the masculine gender when referring to the Spirit? Because Paul knows of no Trinity. There is only God the Father and the Lord Jesus Christ that he serves and worships, as he already indicated in the opening verses of this letter: "Paul, called to be an apostle of Christ Jesus by the will of God, and our brother Sosthenes . . . Grace and peace to you from God our Father and the Lord Jesus Christ" (1 Cor 1:1, 3).

It is important to realize that Jesus *asks the Father* to send the Spirit; he does not ask the Spirit directly. Jesus nowhere prays to the Spirit as being a distinct personage alongside the Father. More than this, even though the

Spirit does come as the second Advocate, it is not included with those *two persons who will love the believers and will come to make their home with the believers:* "Whoever has my commands and keeps them is the one who loves me. The one who loves me will be loved by my Father, and I too will love them and show myself to them" (John 14:21), and, "Jesus replied, 'Anyone who loves me will obey my teaching. My Father will love them, and we will come to them and make our home with them'" (John 14:23).

In the great high priestly prayer of the Messiah found in John chapter 17, Jesus discloses the important and critical truth that the only objects of the faith that will save a person from just damnation *are the two persons of God the Father and Jesus Christ who was sent by God the Father,* as Jesus says, "Now this is eternal life: that they know you, the only true God, and Jesus Christ, whom you have sent" (John 17:3; and see John 14:1). Here, there is no Trinity honored, nor is the belief in the Trinity required for eternal life. When the trinitarians insist that a belief in the Trinity is essential to saving faith and fellowship in the evangelical body of Christ, that is to make Jesus a liar, who said that eternal life is the knowing of only the two persons of God the Father and Jesus Christ whom he has sent. The obtaining of eternal life consists only in the humble fleeing to, and clinging to, both the one true God, Yahweh of the Old Testament, and the Messiah he has sent, Jesus Christ. The Holy Spirit is shamefully omitted. Even after promising the gift of the Spirit as a second Advocate who will remain with the disciples, when Jesus prays his great prayer in John 17, he addresses the Father six times but never addresses the Spirit as a distinct divine person to be prayed to in a supposed Trinity. No Trinity is known or honored by Jesus. The Spirit is shamefully omitted.

But the Holy Spirit is sent both *by the Father and in the name of Jesus* as the second Advocate for the church (John 14:26), and the Holy Spirit is sent by Jesus *from the Father* (John 15:26). It is important to notice that the sending ones are interchangeable due to the incarnation of the Deity in Jesus. Jesus can only send the Spirit because he is the God-man, who is merely *extending his divine being, which is the Father living in him* (see John 14:9–11). We read in the book of Revelation of the glorious Lord Jesus who both "holds" and then wields the "seven spirits of God" throughout the world (Rev 3:1; Rev 5:6). But these two sending ones are the two natures united in the one person of Jesus. When the Father is said to send the Spirit, this should be naturally understood *as any mention in the Old Testament of God pouring out his Spirit.* But when the man, Jesus, says he will send the Spirit, he adds immediately the qualifying statement (which implies the important distinction of the human and divine natures) that this is an extension of the Father, rather than the introduction of another distinct divine person.

When Jesus says he will ask the Father to send "another" Advocate (John 14:16–17), he immediately reminds the disciples that though the world cannot appreciate the invisible working of the Spirit of God, *they, the disciples, already know "it"* because the Spirit *already remains with them and will continue to be with them*. The Greek phrase (*en humin*) used by John usually means "among you," rather than the favored interpretation of the trinitarians as "inside you," as though Jesus was saying something new about the Spirit's impending indwelling the disciples. The Spirit had already made them alive to God and has so far remained with them and will continue to *be among them*. Jesus puts it simply as a replacement advocate companionship in verse 16: "be with you forever" (*hina meth humon eis ton aiona ai*); that is, because the physical man Jesus cannot remain with them on earth until the coming age. This is the reason for "another advocate"— one that can remain with every disciple everywhere, for the purpose of the new church's defense of the Messiah.

It is worth repeating that it is important to realize that Jesus said the disciples *already knew about the Spirit*—as the empowering presence of God—because Jesus *was not saying anything new regarding the reality of the Spirit of God*, when speaking of the coming dispensation, than what they would have known as faithful students of the Mosaic revelation and the writings of the Hebrew prophets. What Jesus said that was new was the *new role of advocacy in the new church age* concerning the vindication of the Messiah. When Jesus says the Father will send "another" Advocate, *he is speaking as the man, Jesus, the prophesied Messiah*. This means he speaks as the one with the human nature who cannot be omnipresent in the world, but that the other Paraclete can be omnipresent because it is the very same Spirit of God that would have been known throughout the revelation of the Old Testament, who can work supernaturally and everywhere.

6

John the Apostle

THE COLLECTIVE BODY OF writings by the apostle John, consisting of the Gospel, the three Letters, and the Revelation of Jesus Christ, will now be considered in this study of Israel's Messiah. Ironically, these Johannine scriptures are regarded by the trinitarians as containing the strongest evidence for the dogma of the Trinity. But the reality is that these scriptures have the strongest evidence that Jesus did not know or reveal anything about the myth of the Trinity.

John's writings contain, naturally, one consistent teaching but which is expressed with different phrasings or styles between the different genres. The Letters have a more concise and earthy style of writing than the Gospel or the Revelation, which renders his message in the Letters more accessible to the ordinary reader. Consequently, the First Letter of John is the key to understanding some of the more elaborate and poetic phrasing of especially the Gospel of John. The Gospel's style is more susceptible to misreading, especially if one does not know how to read it in the original Greek language and does not regard the antecedent theology of the Old Testament. However, even the Greek language of the Gospel is much clearer as to what John means to say and helps us see how he utilizes certain terms and phraseology.

How an author uses a term in his own writings is critical and decisive for a correct understanding of an author's message or teaching. It is extremely important to understand how John uses certain terms in his writings to ascertain the *true content* of Johannine theology. In my opinion, the Trinity myth arose because especially Gentile theologians, in the early church soon after the apostolic era, had carelessly read the terms that John the Jewish apostle uses. These early Gentile converts to Christianity came from the Greco-Roman cultural background which was drunk with polytheism and, therefore, already more comfortable to let their imagination develop the notion of a complex Godhead due to the critical misreading of the prologue to the Gospel of John, as will be shown. These theologians had evidently disregarded both the intended Jewish sense and John's personal style, which then became the ultimate misreading, giving rise to the dogma of a complex Godhead starting with the idea of the "eternal Logos."

In my estimation, the first three Gospels in the Bible are mainly concerned to demonstrate that the Jewish man Jesus is the prophesied Messiah, fulfilling Old Testament prophecies. Consequently, in all the Gospels we see the unbelief and rejection of the claims of the Messiah by most of the Jews of his day even throughout the growth of the early church. But the Gospel of John is concerned not only with proving Jesus to be the prophesied Messiah but has the honor of *more directly proclaiming the truth of the incarnation of God bodily in the Lord Jesus,* which was intimated by the Old Testament prophets. However, John affirms the deity of the Messiah with a beautiful consistency with the Torah revelation, as we have been studying, and not according to the myth of the Trinity at all.

The very root of the notion of a complex Godhead is found in the prologue to the Gospel of John, especially the first three verses, which are inevitably misread by Christian theologians who should know better. Such basic rules of scripture reading and interpretation are: the minding of how an author uses a term himself, and what are the contexts in which his terms or statements are found, and what is the antecedent Old Testament theological background respecting the topic of the author? All of these rules are *shamefully violated* when it comes to the trinitarian reading and interpretation of the prologue of John.

In John 1:1–18, we have the prologue to the Gospel of John. Many New Testament scholars would agree that the prologue is written as an *inclusio,* where the passage mirrors itself and concludes with repeated ideas. The first verse mirrors the last verse. What is extremely important to bear in mind, and what I hope to demonstrate, is that John is writing as an Hebraic Jew—not as a Hellenized Jew who would be fond of Greek philosophy such as the famous Jew named Philo who was heavily influenced by Greek philosophy rather than the pure word of God in the Old Testament. All of the metaphors and typology utilized by John's unique style of writing is derived from the Old Testament. When John uses the term "logos," he does not imply any Greek philosophical nuance. Rather, he means the common, simple Hebraic sense of "communication," or "message." John's unique style of writing includes the many famous metaphors for the Lord Jesus, such as "Word," "Light," "Lamb," "Door," "Shepherd," "Bread," and "Morningstar."

In this passage, John was writing about the significant event of the appearance of two men on the scene of history: both the forerunner of the Messiah, John the baptizer, and the Lord Jesus himself. In the Greek language of this passage, the intention of John's writing becomes clearer. Unfortunately, our English versions, including the breaks of the paragraphs, lose the manner of writing in the original Greek language, which would help us to see the rather simple ideas that he was communicating about the significant event of both the forerunner of the Messiah, John the baptizer, and the Lord Jesus himself. These simple ideas concerning these two men are perfectly consistent with the other three "synoptic" Gospels, *which know nothing about an "eternal Logos," or "eternal Son,"* existing from the eternal past alongside God the Father as a member of a supposed complex Godhead! Would not such a momentous fact of the Godhead be mentioned by all of the Gospel accounts rather than be omitted?!

The first verse of the prologue can be seen as the actual introductory statement, which emphasizes that *at the start of Jesus' gospel ministry there were some basic facts about the Messiah:* that he was the *consummate communication* from God, that he was *perfectly devoted* to God, and that *God made his consummate appearance in the person of the Messiah.*

Then the following verses 2 through 5 address the appearance of the Messiah. And then the following verses 6 through 8 address the appearance of the forerunner of the Messiah, John the baptizer. Then the following verses 9 through 18 address the effects and the responses to the appearance of God in the Messiah Jesus. The last verse of the prologue restates the ministry of the unique Son of God, as the final and consummate prophet, in his revealing who the Father really is for the purpose of redemption.

The paragraphs addressing both Jesus and John begin with John's style of introduction of persons with this formula: sometimes he first says something significant about a person, then he will add the word denoting "this one," using the specific Greek term *houtos*. It is not the term for the simple pronoun "he" as the English versions usually translate it and which obscures his style because it could simply be referring to God as well as a man. In the Gospel of John especially, *houtos* is a term which always *distinguishes between human persons, or even things, but never points out the Deity as distinguished from a man.* So, John writes, according to my translation, "In the beginning was the Word, and the Word was toward God, and God was the Word. *This one* was in the beginning toward God" (John 1:1-2). Again, when he introduces John the baptizer, he says, according to my translation, "There was a man sent from God whose name was John. *This one* came as a witness to testify concerning that light, etc." (John 1:6–7.) John uses this phrasing often (John 1:2, 7; John 3:2; John 4:47; John 6:52; John 9:24, 33; 1 John 5:6, 20; 2 John 7, 9. The main point is that the usage of this Greek word helps us to see that John's Gospel prologue is *discussing two individual men* rather than making the needless distinction between John the baptizer and a supposed eternal divine being, as the trinitarians insist.

In the prologue to the Gospel of John, the most critical portion to correctly read is the first three verses, which incorporates the introduction of the first man, Jesus. And the most important word to correctly understand is the term "beginning." We need to ask *what beginning* is John speaking about? Then the second most important word to correctly understand is the term "with." It seems from the early second century AD of the church age, this first term "beginning" began to be carelessly assumed to mean the beginning of time, and, by implication, the eternal past. Part of the misreading seems to be because these first two words of the English "in the beginning" that is in the original Greek (*en arche*) are the same as the first two words in the Greek translation of the book of Genesis (*en arche*) in the Septuagint version of the Old Testament. With this careless assumption of similarity, it was natural to think "in the beginning" referred to the eternal past, and so seemed to indicate that the phrase "in the beginning was the Word" meant to reveal an eternal divine person alongside God from the eternal past. Then it was apparently assumed that this "eternal Logos" was the very "eternal Son of God" who came "from heaven."

The mistaken meaning of "beginning" completely ignores the *actual sense in which John uses it throughout his writings.* All trinitarians violate this basic hermeneutical rule, which demands *how did the author use a term in question.* The prevailing historic disregard of this principle is astonishing and shameful. The usual dishonest efforts of the trinitarians to understand this term "beginning" would seek for *a sense outside the writings of John,* such as the beginning of creation in Genesis 1:1, and the companionship of Wisdom with God in Proverbs 8:22–31. But there is no need for this desperate reaching when John is clear how he intends the word in the contexts of his writings. Also, because of the mistaken meaning of "beginning," the trinitarians found a supposed statement of eternal origin for the Son in Psalm 2:7, where Yahweh says he has adopted his son. They then speculated that the Son was *eternally begotten*—without a beginning. But the Jewish nation always understood this verse to regard the earthly Davidic king at his installation, according to the plain revelation of 2 Samuel 7:14. And the Jewish apostles *never affirm such trinitarian insight about the person of Jesus.* Not even one trinitarian proof-text is ever discussed by the apostles in the New Testament.

According to the New Testament, the baptism and commencement of the public ministry of the Messiah Jesus *constitutes the beginning of the gospel* (Mark 1:1–14; Luke1:1–4; Luke 3:1–23; Acts 1:21–22). The consistent sense of the term "beginning" that John uses is the sense that refers to the beginning of the first century gospel events. For example, in 1 John 2:7–8, John reminds his readers of the new commandment of love which Jesus gave to his disciples during his ministry on earth (see John 13:34). John often refers to the beginning of the new commandment, or even to the whole gospel message, when writing to a later generation of believers (1 John 1:1; 1 John 2:7; 1 John 2:13–14; 1 John 3:11; 2 John 5–6). In John's Gospel, Jesus refers to the fellowship of his disciples as being from the beginning of his ministry (John 6:64; John 15:27; John 16:4). The only exception would be when the Devil is mentioned as being a murderer or sinner "from the beginning" (John 8:44; 1 John 3:8). Either this means the beginning of man's creation (since Satan was an upright angel when the angels were first created), or probably the beginning of Jesus' ministry due to the unique style of John's writing.

It is helpful and important to notice that the first verse of the First Letter of John also opens with a "beginning" statement that is similar to the prologue to the Gospel of John but which includes the important clues that John is speaking about the beginning of the gospel ministry of the Lord Jesus. John immediately adds the testimony of personal encounter, saying, "which we have heard, which we have seen with our eyes, which we have looked at and our hands have touched—this we proclaim concerning the Word of life." He emphasizes the physicality of the man Jesus. He says nothing about an eternal divine being who existed alongside the Father. Also, he begins his statement with the neuter term, which can refer to either a person or a thing. Later, with a masculine pronoun, John mentions that the early generation of believers had known the Lord Jesus from the beginning of the gospel in verses 13 and 14 of the second chapter. Also, in the First Letter, John calls the Lord Jesus, whom he has seen and touched, the longer title of "the Word of life," which is also confirmed about the Messiah in the book of Revelation, stating, "He is dressed in a robe dipped in blood, and his name is the Word of God" (Rev 19:13).

Another reason to jettison the notion that John is introducing the "eternal Logos" is that there is no satisfying explanation the trinitarians can provide as to why only the second member of the Trinity should be described as existing from the "beginning" and not the Father or the Holy Spirit. Are they not also from the "beginning"? Was not the Father existing from the "beginning" also? Was not the Holy Spirit existing from the "beginning" also? And more than this, why does John suggest only the older generation of Christian believers (the "fathers") knew him who existed from the "beginning"? When the trinitarians maintain this notion, it becomes silly to read John's Letter saying that *only some* believers knew him who was from the "beginning" in 1 John 2:13–14. Did not all the members of the church know him who existed from the "beginning"? Rather, the better interpretation of these verses is that the older generation of Christian believers either knew the gospel message from the start of its proclamation, or possibly even knew the Lord Jesus himself. The Greek literally says, "knew [either the one or the thing] *from* the beginning," but does not say, "knew the one *who was* from the beginning." The reality is that the elements of dishonesty, circular reasoning, and stupidity are always present in the preaching of the dogma of the Trinity, which simply neglects the antecedent Jewish understanding of both the person of Yahweh, the prophesied Messiah, and the activity of the Holy Spirit.

In the prologue, the second most important word to correctly understand is the term "with." The term "with" is the usual English Bible translation. But this is inaccurate. The Greek term is *pros,* which usually means "to," or "toward." It means a directional movement toward something or facing something, but not an original companionship; nor a tandem, co-etaneous existence. So, when John says the Word was "with" God, he is actually saying that the Word was *toward* God, probably in the sense of being thoroughly devoted to God, as well as implying a relation between two real entities (or beings), and not as the murky distinction between the one-essence members of the triune Godhead; and John's expression using "toward" may have derived from the statements about the Messiah that expressed complete dedicated service to God in Isaiah 53:2 ("before him"), and Micah 5:2 ("for me"), and Zechariah 13:7 ("to me"). This sense can be illustrated by its use elsewhere in scripture. For examples, John says we have an advocate *toward* the Father (1 John 2:1), and Paul's prayer is said *toward* God (Romans 10:1). Neither of these can be correctly read as a joint, tandem experience shared between the parties.

With the foregoing terms being correctly understood according to John's nuanced meanings, the passage is then read to say, "At the beginning of the gospel, there was the Messiah Jesus (who, being the consummate communication from God, is metaphorically called "the Word"), and he who was the *Word* was completely devoted in loving service to God." John immediately adds the extremely important clause which reveals that God was the Word, meaning God was actually incarnate in the Word. Then in verse 3, the following declaration (where the trinitarians misread the supposed creative agency of the *Word*) should be correctly understood to mean that because God was actually that *Word,* being incarnate in Jesus, *the unique divine glory of creation is then credited to the Messiah Jesus.* John restates this fact of the credit of creation about Jesus later in verse 10, "He was in the world, and though the world was made through him, the world did not recognize him."

This *incarnational language* (or "code," if you will) is used in only a few texts (see 1 Cor 8:6; Col 1:16; Heb 1:2, 10). But more often in both the Old Testament and New Testament, God the Father of the redeemed is the *sole* creator of all things, as these verses demonstrate: "This is the account of the heavens and the earth when they were created, when the LORD God made the earth and the heavens" (Gen 2:4); "For in six days the LORD made the heavens and the earth, the sea, and all that is in them, but he rested on the seventh day. Therefore the LORD blessed the Sabbath day and made it holy" (Exod 20:11); "Where were you when I laid the earth's foundation?" (Job 38:4); "When I consider your heavens, the work of your fingers, the moon and the stars, which you have set in place" (Ps 8:3); "The earth is the LORD's, and everything in it, the world, and all who live in it; for he founded it on the seas and established it on the waters" (Ps 24:1–2); "Before he made the world or its fields or any of the dust of the earth" (Prov 8:26): "This is what God the LORD says—the Creator of the heavens, who stretches them out, who spreads out the earth with all that springs from it, who gives breath to its people, and life to those who walk on it" (Isa 42:5); "It is I who made the earth and created mankind on it. My own hands stretched out the heavens; I marshaled their starry hosts," and, "For this is what the LORD says—he who created the heavens, he is God; he who fashioned and made the earth, he founded it; he did not create it to be empty, but formed it to be inhabited—he says: 'I am the LORD, and there is no other'" (Isa 45:12, 18); " 'Haven't you read,' he replied, 'that at the beginning the Creator made them male and female'" (Matt 19:4); "But at the beginning of creation God 'made them male and female'" (Mark 10:6); "When they heard this, they raised their voices together in prayer to God. 'Sovereign Lord,' they said, 'you made the heavens and the earth and the sea, and everything in them'" (Acts 4:24); "The God who made the world and everything in it is the Lord of heaven and earth and does not live in temples built by human hands" (Acts 17:24); "'Who has ever given to God, that God should repay them?' For from him and through him and for him are all things" (Rom 11:35–36); "Yet for us there is but one God, the Father, from whom all things came" (1 Cor 8:6); "In bringing many sons and daughters to glory, it was fitting that God, for whom and through whom everything exists" (Heb 2:10); "By faith we understand that the universe was formed at God's command, so that what is seen was not made out of what was visible" (Heb 11:3); "But they deliberately forget that long ago by God's word the heavens came into being and the earth was formed out of water and by water" (2 Pet 3:5); " You are worthy, our Lord and God, to receive glory and honor and power, for you created all things, and by your will they were created and have their being" (Rev 4:11).

Then, in verse 14 of the prologue, which is the famous incarnational statement being misread as though the supposed "eternal Word" was *metamorphosed* into a man, we actually have a simple assertion of the real humanity of the Messiah during his days on earth (see Col 2:9; Heb 2:14–17; 1 John 4:2; 2 John 7), contrary to the heretical Docetists who insisted on a mere apparition of the Messiah. The Greek language supports this simple interpretation: *Kai ho logos sarx egeneto kai eskanosen en hamin.* The term for "flesh" is in the emphatic position of the sentence, which stresses the thought that Jesus, when he had come, *occurred as a real human being of flesh and blood.* The term *egeneto* means "became or happened," and is the simple idea of *occurrence,* and does not necessarily indicate a supernatural transformation. An example is when the Lord Jesus is described as the one "who died and came to life again" (Rev 2:8). There the words are *hos egeneto nekros,* meaning, "who became dead." This reading of verse 14 is also supported by the First and Second Letter of John, where he more plainly states what this verse is conveying. John says, "This is how you can recognize the Spirit of God: Every spirit that acknowledges that *Jesus Christ has come in the flesh* is from God" (1 John 4:2); and again, "I say this because many deceivers, who do not acknowledge *Jesus Christ as coming in the flesh,* have gone out into the world" (2 John 7). In these verses, John is asserting the important fact of the real humanity of the Lord Jesus. He is not teaching that a supposed "eternal Logos" metamorphosized into a human being, according to the usual misreading of the trinitarians.

In verse 17 of the prologue, John finally mentions who he has been speaking of by his name— "Jesus Christ." And it should be noticed that early in the prologue, John asserts that "In him was life, and that life was the light of all mankind" (v 4). It would be absurd to think that only the supposed second member of the Trinity was the "light of all mankind" rather than all of God. But as has been shown, John is referring to a certain man called the Word, and he states in his First Letter the fact that eternal life is provided by God through the ministry of his Messiah, and locating it only in him, saying, "And this is the testimony: God has given us eternal life, *and this life is in his Son*" (1 John 5:11). And the Messiah himself implies that the reference to "life as the light of mankind" is to be located only in his human person, the man Jesus: "When Jesus spoke again to the people, he said, 'I am the light of the world. Whoever follows me will never walk in darkness, but will have the light of life'" (John 8:12).

In verse 18 of the prologue, we have the conclusion of the whole prologue, and this verse serves as an end-cap mirror to the first verse. The first
verse announced the Lord Jesus as the consummate communication from
God, who reveals both the true kingdom and salvation of God provided
through the loving acceptance of the Sent One. Jesus is the uniquely begotten (not the "only begotten") Son of God who only knows the Father
(see Matt 11:27) due to the incarnation of God within him. Jesus lies *in the
bosom of only the Father* (NIV: "is in closest relationship with the Father"),
and it is *only the Father that Jesus reveals to mankind* (NIV: "has made him
known"). The Son lies in the bosom of the Father, and so is uniquely quali-
fied to explain the Father. Jesus reveals nothing about a supposed Trinity of
persons but only the Father, as he later affirms: "Righteous Father, though
the world does not know you, I know you, and they know that you have
sent me. *I have made you known to them*" (John 17:25–26). If there is a real
Trinity, it is absurd to think that Jesus is in closest relationship with only the
Father and only reveals the Father but not the Holy Spirit, which is the delimitation of this verse. This omission is shameful and cannot be explained
in any satisfying way by the trinitarians.

We never read the title "the Word" again in the Gospel of John because
it was just one of a series of metaphorical titles that John gives to the man
Jesus. It does not signify a supposed eternal being alongside the Father. The
other apostles never refer to Jesus as "the Word" in their New Testament
writings, nor do they show any knowledge of an "eternal Logos." John calls
Jesus "the Word" precisely because he brings a final message from God. This
fact is emphasized in the eighth chapter of the Gospel: "'Who are you?' they
asked. 'Just what *I have been telling you from the beginning*,' Jesus replied. 'I
have much to say in judgment of you. But he who sent me is trustworthy,
and *what I have heard from him I tell the world*'" (John 8:25–26).

If the prologue of the Gospel of John is correctly read and interpreted,
then we will understand that whenever the "Son" is spoken of in the writings
of John, he is referring not to the traditional trinitarian idea of an "eternal
Logos" or "eternal Son" but to the man Jesus, in whom Yahweh—who is the
Creator, the unique Father of the Messiah, and the Father of the redeemed
people—is incarnate bodily. John knows or says nothing about the trinitarian notion of an "eternal Son," who is supposedly "co-equal" to the Father,
because then that would mean the Son having had an underived divine authority over mankind and creation prior to his appearance on earth. But if
we pay attention to the words of Jesus in the forthcoming chapters of John's
Gospel, then we will see *that* was not the case for him. For now, it might be
helpful to view verses 1–11 of John's prologue schematically, from the NIV:

1 In the beginning [of the gospel] was the Word, and the Word was [toward] God, and the Word was God.

2 [This one] was [toward] God in the beginning [of the gospel].

3 Through him all things were made; without him nothing was made that has been made (= v 10).

4 In him was life, and that life was the light of all mankind.

5 The light shines in the darkness, and the darkness has not overcome it.

6 There was a man sent from God whose name was John.

7 [This one] came as a witness to testify concerning that light, so that through him all might believe.

8 He himself was not the light; he came only as a witness to the light.

9 The true light that gives light to everyone was coming into the world.

10 He was in the world, and though the world was made through him, the world did not recognise him.

11 He came to that which was his own, but his own did not receive him.

According to the testimony of the Messiah, all of the divine authority of the Messiah is a *derived* authority from God: the authority for his redemptive ministry, the authority to judge the world, the authority to give eternal life, the authority to found and head the church, and the authority to rule the universe. In the passage in John 5:19–30, the Messiah declares, in so many words, that his divine authority—which is supernatural power and right—was *given to him* by Yahweh, the Father. It was given in the sense that he could *do nothing by himself* if it were not given to him. It is not the absurd, pretended sense of the "eternal Son" showing loving deference, as though the "eternal Son" was merely being polite. There are no empty, meaningless, misleading words in the scriptures. *To give* authority is the appropriate role of the Creator: "It is God who judges: He brings one down, he exalts another" (Ps 75:7), and *to receive* anything good is the appropriate role of a created being: "To this John replied, 'A person can receive only what is given them from heaven'" (John 3:27).

The original inability of Jesus refers to his humanity because such authority and ability is never to be found inherent in a created being such as an ordinary man. Jesus understands this. That is why he declares his disclaimers concerning his calling: "The Son *can do nothing by himself*; he can do only what he sees his Father doing, because whatever the Father does the Son also does" (John 5:19); "If I testify about myself, *my testimony is not true*" (John 5:31). Such disclaimers would be absurd from the mouth of God about himself. Yahweh is never reluctant to declare his glory and authority. Therefore, to suggest the "eternal Son" would practice such insincere self-abasement is simply ridiculous.

Some of the authority given to the Messiah is mentioned by Jesus in the passage we are looking at: "For the Father loves the Son and shows him all he does" (v 20); "For just as the Father raises the dead and gives them life, even so the Son gives life to whom he is pleased to give it" (v 21); "Moreover, the Father judges no one, but has entrusted all judgment to the Son, that all may honor the Son just as they honor the Father. Whoever does not honor the Son does not honor the Father, who sent him" (vv 22–23); "For as the Father has life in himself, so he has granted the Son also to have life in himself. And he has given him authority to judge because he is the Son of Man" (vv 26–27). In these last words, we see that Jesus recognizes himself as a man. The phrase "son of man" derives from the Old Testament scriptures, and always and everywhere means an ordinary human being of flesh and blood.

In the passage in Mark 2:1–12, the Messiah was accused of blasphemy by some of the teachers of the Law when he declared forgiveness of sins for a paralyzed man who looked to Jesus for help. It seems reasonable that the one who has authority to judge all mankind (God) is also the one who can forgive sins. Therefore, when Jesus asserts in John 5:22 that the Father has entrusted the authority to judge all mankind to the Son of Man, then that would mean he has been given the authority to forgive sins on earth as well. But this authority to forgive sins on earth—even as a man—is not a proof-text for the eternal sonship of Jesus because it is divine authority given to "the Son of Man" (Mark 2:10; and see Matthew 9:6 and Luke 5:24).

When we keep in mind the recognized fact that Jesus regards himself as a man rather than as a divine "eternal Son," we then can understand correctly how he was *divinely commissioned* to speak for God as well as provide atonement for God's people. This is emphasized in the eighth chapter of John's Gospel. The Messiah describes himself throughout the Gospel as the Sent One. Whenever Jesus says that he has come "down from heaven" and "sent into the world," these expressions are metaphorical, and are not to be mistakenly read—as the trinitarians are fond of doing with shameful lack of hermeneutical scholarship—as though these were meaning an actual locomotive movement from a point in heaven (where God is) down to earth. These are mainly John's phraseology, and he uses them for other people and things as well. Such expressions referring to a person "coming from God" or "coming down from heaven" or "sent from God" or "sent from heaven" or "come into the world" simply mean that person has been divinely decreed to appear on the scene of history, or divinely commissioned, or something has been divinely granted. It does not mean a person has come from the very presence of God in heaven down to earth! Moreover, the idea is absurd because no human being ever originates in heaven. Some examples are: "There was a man sent from God whose name was John" (John 1:6); "He came to Jesus at night and said, 'Rabbi, we know that you are a teacher who has come from God" (John 3:2); "After the people saw the sign Jesus performed, they began to say, 'Surely this is the Prophet who is to come into the world'" (John 6:14); "A woman giving birth to a child has pain because her time has come; but when her baby is born she forgets the anguish because of her joy that a child is born into the world" (John 16:21); " 'You are a king, then!' said Pilate. Jesus answered, 'You say that I am a king. In fact, the reason I was born and came into the world is to testify to the truth. Everyone on the side of truth listens to me'" (John 18:37).

God is never sent as a servant, but a man is sent as a servant. Even when God sends his Spirit, it is not as a servant *per se* but merely the sharing of his personal presence for direct interaction as the Deity with his people. But the Messiah was sent as other prophets and apostles who served God, just as he acknowledges about himself before the Father: "As you sent me into the world, I have sent them into the world. For them I sanctify myself, that they too may be truly sanctified" (John 17:18–19). When Jesus speaks of his calling and ministry, he always describes himself in terms that are only appropriate for a man and not for a divine being: "'Who are you?' they asked. 'Just what I have been telling you from the beginning,' Jesus replied. 'I have much to say in judgment of you. But he who sent me is trustworthy, and what I have heard from him I tell the world.' They did not understand that he was telling them about his Father. So Jesus said, 'When you have lifted up the Son of Man, then you will know that I am he and that I do nothing on my own but speak just what the Father has taught me. The one who sent me is with me; he has not left me alone, for I always do what pleases him'" (John 8:25–29).

Although Jesus regarded himself as a man, he knew that he was more than an ordinary man. Jesus also *knew that Yahweh, God Almighty, was incarnate in himself.* He knew that he was *uniquely begotten* through miraculous birth, and without defilement of sin, and for the permanent incarnation of Deity. His appearance was predestined, and he was raised up providentially for the fulfillment of messianic prophecy, divine redemption, and covenant promise. He was *personally conscious* of, and *openly testified* to, the fact that God, the Father, was living in him bodily in a special and permanent union for the sake of his people's redemption and the glorification of his human person. It is as the apostle Paul concisely writes about Jesus Christ in his letter to the Philippians: that although he, the man, consciously existed in the role of God and did not regard this equality with God as inappropriate, in great humility he "emptied" himself so that the Godward aspect of his person was *somehow passive* during his life on earth, thereby taking the role of a mere servant of God for the sake of his mission regarding the will of God for his people's redemption (see Phil 2:5–8).

In the Gospel of John especially do we read that the Messiah, Jesus, knew that he came as God Almighty; and in this gospel especially do we read that Jesus always describes this incarnation in terms of the union of the two natures, the divine and the human, *and which involves only two individual personages.*

The single divine person is, of course, Yahweh, the Father of Israel and the redeemed people. When the scriptures announce through the prophets and evangelists the coming of the Messiah, these announce the coming of Yahweh himself, the Lord of the Old Testament era, as we read in the Gospel of Mark 1:1–3: "The beginning of the good news about Jesus the Messiah, the Son of God, as it is written in Isaiah the prophet: 'I will send my messenger ahead of you, who will prepare your way'—'a voice of one calling in the wilderness, Prepare the way for the Lord, make straight paths for him.'" The "Lord," here, is Yahweh. He is coming.

Regarding himself, the man Jesus in whom Yahweh has finally accomplished this announced coming bodily, he declares that he had been especially *set apart from the rest of humanity and thereby selected* to be the anointed one who would fulfill the will of God for the sake of the salvation of mankind (John 10:36). The Greek term that John has Jesus use (*hagiasen*) means to set apart for a holy purpose. This would be absurd to apply to the supposed "eternal Son of God." No such separation is needed for God. It is clear from the encounters of Jesus with the unbelieving Jews that they were offended with the implications of Jesus' statements about himself and his unique relationship with God the Father in that he had called God his *own* Father, and also that *by the exercise of divine power, along with the Father, in the keeping of the real sheep of God,* he and the Father were *one presence, one in purpose, and one in powerful activity:* "I and the Father are one" (John 10:30).

The usual trinitarian interpretation of this oneness in verse 30 tends to be said as strictly one essence; that is, a metaphysical unity of essence shared between "God the Father" and "God the Son." But antecedent theology, the wider context of John's Gospel, and the surrounding context of this verse renders that specific trinitarian notion as inaccurate nonsense. It cannot mean one essence because the two natures of human and divine are impossible to be of the same essence. And the scriptures only present the Jewish sense of the divine incarnation, as we have been studying. Yahweh has become incarnate in the man Jesus. The two natures are now united in one person and displayed in the activity of that one person. What is more, the statement of Jesus in this important verse *involves the unity of only the two persons of God the Father and the man Jesus.* No Trinity is honored here. The Holy Spirit is shamefully omitted here, especially when we recall that the Bible teaches that the strength and preservation of the people of God are mediated through the ministry of the Spirit of God poured out on them.

Therefore, we learn two facts, according to the perception of the unbelieving Jews: That Jesus certainly claimed, by implication, that he, a mere man according to outward appearance, made himself equal to God; That Jesus claimed to be God. But with all of these narrative facts it is also clear that this one man claimed to be the one God. Consequently, even by the witness of the unbelieving Jews, we are to *notice only the two persons*: the man Jesus and the singular person God. This was all that the unbelieving Jews noticed. There was no disclosure or discussion of a Trinity whenever Jesus encountered conflict about his person and authority.

According to the Gospel account of John 10:22–39, the Messiah openly declared that he and the Father were "one" (v 30). The Greek term for "one" (*hen*) is the neuter gender and can serve persons or ideas or things. In context, Jesus had just declared how both he and the Father can keep safely their sheep by *their power equally:* "my hand" and "my Father's hand" (vv 28–29). This means that Jesus and the Father act as one, or that they behave as one person. It means that God is incarnate in Jesus, as affirmed by John in his prologue: "the Word was God" (John 1:1). It means that, in a special way, Jesus represents God in his person. This interpretation is confirmed by the perception of the unbelieving Jews who wanted to stone Jesus because he definitely "claimed to be God" (v 33) through his assertions of divine power and the display of God's will and authority through his personal activities.

In the Gospel of John, the Messiah openly declares, and commands that we understand clearly, that *God the Father is incarnate in his person,* and that *he represents God in a real and living way through his person.* The unique language found only in the Gospel of John to describe the incarnation of God is asserted by Jesus in these words: "know and understand that the Father is in me, and I in the Father" (John 10:38). Jesus consistently describes *the union of only the two persons,* which equals the intimate, divine, reciprocal knowledge of only the two persons: "Just as the Father knows me and I know the Father—and I lay down my life for the sheep," and, "I and the Father are one," and, "the Father is in me, and I in the Father" (John 10:15, 30, 38).

When Jesus defends himself to the offended Jews who would stone him for blasphemy, he appeals to Psalm 82, and asserts two facts: their scriptures provide precedence of God calling either angels or men either "gods" or "sons of God," and also another fact that trinitarians never pay attention to—the only true God has only ever designated *created beings* as his "sons." Jesus does not know of, nor honors himself as, the supposed "eternal Son" when he would have the unbelieving Jews to "know and understand" his human role as the incarnate God. More than this, Jesus (the manward aspect of the God-man) says, "I am God's Son" only *by virtue of the incarnation of God in him*: "Do not believe me unless I do the works of my Father. But if I do them, even though you do not believe me, believe the works, that you may know and understand that the Father is in me, and I in the Father" (John 10:37–38).

The Messiah will continue to emphasize the fact of the incarnation of God in his person to his disciples. One of his disciples, Philip, asks Jesus to somehow show the disciples the God of Israel and so that would be satisfying, if less than coming to God: "Philip said, 'Lord, show us the Father and that will be enough for us'" (John 14:8). Now, Philip was a godly Jew and a fellow disciple with those whom Jesus had called to attend him as their rabbi. But Philip does not know anything about a Trinity, nor does he wish to see the other members of a supposed Trinity. As a biblical Jew, he only knows that Yahweh was known as the Father of Israel and therefore *requests to see him alone*. Jesus confirms this theological understanding—not by correcting and informing him of a deeper revelation of the supposed Trinity but by asserting that if Philip has seen Jesus, he has seen the God of Israel: "Jesus answered: 'Don't you know me, Philip, even after I have been among you such a long time? Anyone who has seen me has seen the Father. How can you say, Show us the Father?" (John 14:9). Then Jesus explains, with the unique *mutual indwelling*, saying, "Believe me when I say that I am in the Father and the Father is in me" (John 14:11). According to Jesus, the fulfillment of the prophesied incarnation of God in the son given to Israel consists of only the Father of Israel becoming incarnate bodily in the man Jesus. Jesus also explains his human role of being the incarnate God as the Father "living" or "remaining" in him: "Don't you believe that I am in the Father, and that the Father is in me? The words I say to you I do not speak on my own authority. Rather, it is the Father, living in me, who is doing his work" (John 14:10). However difficult it may be to comprehend the divine incarnation in the person of Jesus, it is clear from the plain text that *the incarnation involves only the single person Father of Israel and the man Jesus*.

The Messiah declared in what sense he is the Son of God by asserting that he is the man who was predestined for the incarnation of God. Jesus also declared himself to be the unique "Son of Man." Biblically, this phrase, "son of man," always means an ordinary man of flesh and blood, or a son of Adam. And biblically, "son of God" meant specifically the anointed king of

Israel, or generally, a creature who was produced by the supernatural will of God rather than the ordinary means of procreation, such as Adam or even the angels in heaven. But nowhere in scripture is suggested the pagan, polytheistic sense of a divine "son of God" who would have been derived somehow directly from a deity. But when Jesus constantly refers to himself as the Son of Man, he means the unique scriptural sense that we learn in the prophecy of Daniel 7:9–14. There, as we have seen, a son of man is presented to God who then gives this man the glory and dominion of God, which belongs only to God. This amazing grant is the revelation of inspired scripture. It is in this sense that the Messiah appeared as the Son of Man and in which sense Jesus regarded himself. Not only meaning this term's bare meaning, of one who has flesh and blood, but also meaning the unique one to whom will be given the glory and dominion of God.

He is a real man, having been born from a mother's womb, having his own soul and the accompanying will and feelings of a real human being, with its corporal limitations. He is susceptible to sorrow and insult, spitting and whipping, fatigue and hunger, nails and dying, all the while God being united to him and incarnate in him bodily. But he was uniquely commissioned by God, which is expressed uniquely by John's writing style as the man who "came down from heaven" (John 6:41). No other Gospel writer designates Jesus as such. They are not aware of the crass locomotive notion of the trinitarians suggesting Jesus having come directly from heaven to earth. Paul and the Synoptic Gospel writers, consistent with the Hebrew prophets, only know Jesus as having been born of a woman. Jesus declares that he is the "man from heaven," but only in the *same metaphorical sense* as being the "bread from heaven." "At this the Jews there began to grumble about him because he said, 'I am the bread that came down from heaven'" (John 6:41). This is no more literal than when Jesus declares, "I am the bread of life" (John 6:48). These expressions simply refer to the divine commission of the Messiah, which provides eternal life. Also, the silly notion that "Son of Man" really means a divine being having originated in heaven has been hatched only by the unscriptural imaginations of both the intertestamental Jews and the post-New Testament early church.

In the unique writings of John, we must keep the entire corpus in mind as well as good reasoning. Therefore, when we read Jesus saying, "I came from the Father and entered the world; now I am leaving the world and going back to the Father" (John 16:28), we must keep in mind all of the antecedent theology of the Old Testament, which we have studied, as well as the wider context of all the writings of John, if we would ascertain the correct sense of John's unique expressions of the declarations of the Messiah. Therefore, Jesus is simply declaring that his birth and life were divinely predestined and commissioned by the Father, but then he will go to the Father when he is resurrected and seated at the right hand of God.

The Greek language is helpful because the English versions can be misleading. The Greek of the second clause (which is more important) is *palin aphiami ton kosmon kai poreuomai pros ton patera*. This reads literally, according to my translation, "again, I remit (or leave) the world and proceed (or go) to the Father." The English makes the clause read as though Jesus was *going back again, or returning,* to the Father (as though his person had literally originated from the very presence of God). But, as a human being, he was never actually there before, as we know from antecedent theology. The term "again" refers to the entire second-clause-phase of his life. Jesus is saying, "Then," or, "now, I will be going to the Father." "Again" regards the additional movement in the second clause. It is used as indicating an additional statement in Matthew 5:33, where Jesus is speaking the sermon on the mount. There, it does not mean to return to something again. The term "back," as it is in the NIV, is additional to the Greek text and probably derived from the Greek word "again," but which undoubtedly comes from the bias of trinitarian dogma. And even if someone were to disagree with this sound interpretation of the verse which I provide, still Jesus knows of no Trinity to go back to. He will be proceeding to only the Father because, as he will go on to say, he is never alone because the Father is always with him—and the Holy Spirit is shamefully omitted (John 16:32).

According to the Gospel of John, when the Messiah appeared, he taught the true kingdom of the God of Israel and also taught *religious truth* concerning a right relationship with God. Jesus taught what was necessary to know and believe in order to be right with God and loved by God. This right relationship involved *religious belief or trust in only two personages having the divine authority over peoples' lives:* the original God of Israel and the additional Lord Jesus Christ, the one whom God had sent into the world for the sake of redemption. This is especially important for the argument of this study. Jesus *commanded certain necessary beliefs* in order to be saved from the wrath of God for sin.

These core necessary beliefs can be summarized as such: Jesus is the prophesied Messiah, and therefore the one whom God had finally sent into the world to preach the true kingdom of God and the necessity to repent of sin and the false understanding of the kingdom of God; Jesus is the final and true Lamb of God who made atonement for sin (which will later also involve the belief in his final priesthood in the order of Melchizedek); Jesus is the one whom God had determined to glorify, and who would share the divine glory with the Father after his resurrection. Therefore, religious belief or trust is to be accorded to the Messiah along with the God of Israel.

The Messiah taught and commanded that Christian believers are now to believe in, trust, obey, and honor Jesus, himself, as well as they believe in, trust, obey, and honor the Father: "That all may *honor the Son just as they honor the Father.* Whoever does not honor the Son does not honor the Father, who sent him" (John 5:23); "Then Jesus cried out, 'Whoever believes in me does not *believe in me only, but in the one who sent me.* The one who looks at me is seeing the one who sent me'" (John 12:44–45); "Do not let your hearts be troubled. *You believe in God; believe also in me*" (John 14:1); "*If you really know me, you will know my Father as well.* From now on, you do know him and have seen him" (John 14:7); "Don't you believe that *I am in the Father, and that the Father is in me?* The words I say to you I do not speak on my own authority. Rather, it is *the Father, living in me,* who is doing his work. *Believe me when I say that I am in the Father and the Father is in me; or at least believe on the evidence of the works themselves*" (John 14:10–11); "Jesus replied, 'Anyone who loves me will obey my teaching. My Father will love them, and *we will come to them and make our home with them*'" (John 14:23); "*Whoever hates me hates my Father as well*" (John 15:23); "Now this is eternal life: *that they know you, the only true God, and Jesus Christ, whom you have sent*" (John 17:3).

John underscores these New Covenant truths of the worship of only the two personages who share the divine glory in his letters: "We proclaim to you what we have seen and heard, so that you also may have fellowship with us. *And our fellowship is with the Father and with his Son, Jesus Christ*" (1 John 1:3); "No one who denies the Son has the Father; *whoever acknowledges the Son has the Father also*" (1 John 2:23); "We know also that the Son of God has come and has given us understanding, so that we may know him who is true. *And we are in him who is true by being in his Son Jesus Christ. He* (Greek: *houtos,* "this one" [Jesus Christ]) *is the true God and eternal life*" (1 John 5:20); "Anyone who runs ahead and does not continue in the teaching of Christ does not have God; whoever continues in the teaching *has both the Father and the Son*" (2 John 9).

The book of John called the Revelation of Jesus Christ provides us with the most descriptive scene of how God is worshiped in heaven. If there is still any doubt whether the dogma of the Trinity is a reality or not, we should be allowed to see, without dimness, such a supposed complex Godhead through the openness of the worship of heaven. But John does not uncover such a Trinity in heaven. John does reveal how God is worshiped by disclosing *the heavenly worship of only the two personages who share the one divine throne, which are God Almighty and the Lamb:* "Then I heard every creature in heaven and on earth and under the earth and on the sea, and all that is in them, saying: *'To him who sits on the throne and to the Lamb* be praise

and honor and glory and power, for ever and ever!' The four living creatures said, 'Amen,' and the elders fell down and worshiped" (Rev 5:13–14);
"After this I looked, and there before me was a great multitude that no one
could count, from every nation, tribe, people and language, standing before
the throne and before the Lamb. They were wearing white robes and were
holding palm branches in their hands. And they cried out in a loud voice:
'Salvation belongs to our God, who sits on the throne, and to the Lamb'" (Rev
7:9–10); "I did not see a temple in the city, because *the Lord God Almighty
and the Lamb are its temple"* (Rev 21:22); "No longer will there be any curse.
The throne of God and of the Lamb will be in the city, and his servants will
serve him" (Rev 22:3).

According to the writings of John, and consistent with the Hebrew
prophets, both the coming of the Jewish Messiah through the womb of an
Israelite mother (and God was that Messiah) and his eventual glorification
occurred during a certain period of time in the present age of human existence. In other words, John does not know anything about a pre-existent
Son who had left the throne of heaven, and then came to earth to live as a
man and accomplish atonement, and then was re-glorified and re-seated on
the throne of heaven. That scenario is pure gratuitous nonsense provoked
by the original misreading of the prologue of John's Gospel. And like the
cult of the rabbis, the trinitarians play fast and loose with the scriptures to
say what they think it should say. But as we have seen in the study of the
messianic prophecies, no such pre-existent "eternal Son" was ever disclosed
by the prophets, and John concurs.

The Messiah taught that he was a man commissioned by the Father
of Israel for the sake of redemption and the glory of God, but that *then he
would be glorified by the Father with the glory that belongs to God alone*: "Jesus replied, 'The hour has come for the Son of Man to be glorified. Very truly
I tell you, unless a kernel of wheat falls to the ground and dies, it remains
only a single seed. But if it dies, it produces many seeds'" (John 12:23–24);
"When he was gone, Jesus said, 'Now the Son of Man is glorified and God
is glorified in him'" (John 13:31); "After Jesus said this, he looked toward
heaven and prayed: 'Father, the hour has come. Glorify your Son, that your
Son may glorify you'" (John 17:1); "And now, Father, glorify me in your
presence with the glory I had with you before the world began" (John 17:5);
"Father, I want those you have given me to be with me where I am, and to
see my glory, the glory you have given me because you loved me before the
creation of the world" (John 17:24).

The request for Jesus' glorification, found in the prayer of John chapter
17, needs to be explained. Trinitarians usually seize the statement in verse 5
as indicating that Jesus *was* equally glorious as the Father *before* the creation

of the world, meaning before the supposed "eternal Son" came to earth, and so it seems to be a proof-text for the Trinity dogma. But this is to disregard all antecedent theology, and all the messianic prophecies, and all the surrounding contexts of John's writings, It is nonsensical for Jesus to say that he had a co-equal glory "before the world began." Had he not supposedly left the throne of heaven much later than before creation, much more recently in the world's existence than that? More importantly, we have already seen that, biblically, whenever the expression "before the creation of the world" is employed, it means something had been divinely predestined to have a real existence or occurrence at some point in history. Jesus is saying that he had a glory *predestined* for him. It was the real, historical granting of this predestined glory that he requests.

This interpretation is supported by Jesus' elaboration of this predestined glory in a verse later in the great prayer (John 17:24), where Jesus says his glory was predestined because of the motivating factor of the Father having loved him "before the creation of the world," just as any Christian believer who has been elected for salvation. And why would the supposed "eternal Son" be loved before the creation of the world only? Was he not loved more recently than that? Was he not loved just before he came to earth?

What is more is that Jesus addresses the Father—and only the Father—six times in this especially important prayer of John chapter 17. No Trinity is honored here. And though Jesus had said that the Spirit of truth will both supernaturally advocate for, and glorify, the Messiah (John 14:16–17, 26; John 15:26; John 16:7–15), Jesus does not address or even acknowledge the Spirit as another concerned personage within the Godhead. The Trinity dogma teaches that the Son of God shares an equal eternal glory with the Father and the Holy Spirit. But Jesus does not acknowledge a supposed shared glory with the Holy Spirit. Jesus does not include the Spirit in the glorious unity of love that encircles the Father, himself, and the believers (John 17:20–23). The Spirit is shamefully omitted.

Another passage above that needs commenting is John 13:31. The trinitarians continually fail to pay attention to what the Messiah actually says, and they always see their hallucinations of the Trinity. Here, Jesus says, "Now the Son of Man is glorified and God is glorified in him." Jesus makes mention of only the two persons who will share the divine throne according to Hebrew prophecy: God and the Son of Man. Two personages arising from two distinct natures. Jesus calls himself the "Son of Man," meaning he is a human being; and he distinguishes himself completely from "God," meaning Yahweh the Father of Israel in heaven. God of course is inherently glorious. But though God was incarnate in Jesus (John 1:1), the man still needed to be glorified (John 17:1). But the Spirit is omitted here. No Trinity is known. Only two persons are mentioned by the Messiah.

According to the book of the Revelation of John's writings, the fact of the scenario displaying that Jesus had not originated from the throne of heaven when he was born—but that he will be seated with God on the throne of heaven after his death and resurrection—is seen in the passage of Revelation 12:1–6. According to the perspective of heaven, Israel is depicted as a glorious woman who then gives birth to "a son, a male child, who 'will rule all the nations with an iron scepter.' And her child was snatched up to God and to his throne." This succinct disclosure reveals simply that a Hebrew man was born from the woman Israel and then snatched up to God and to his throne. No pre-existence of an "eternal Son" is known according to the perspective of heaven. No Trinity fiction is honored here. John's depiction is as simple as David's depiction: "The LORD says to my lord: 'Sit at my right hand until I make your enemies a footstool for your feet.' The LORD will extend your mighty scepter from Zion, saying, 'Rule in the midst of your enemies!'" (Ps 110:1–2).

The writings of the apostles are especially helpful toward our understanding the truth that Jesus, the Son of God, did not originate from heaven as an eternal divine member of the Godhead, but rather was raised up as Moses and other Hebrew prophets were for the sake of doing God's will. Jesus had his origin, as they had, from the womb of a mother. But Jesus' calling was quite different. He was *graced with the name above all names*. All other prophets who were raised up and called to serve the living God served in the name of Yahweh, but Jesus was *given* the name above all names to become, by the express will of Yahweh, Lord of all: "Therefore let all Israel be assured of this: God has made this Jesus, whom you crucified, both Lord and Messiah" (Acts 2:36); "Therefore God exalted him to the highest place and gave him the name that is above every name, that at the name of Jesus every knee should bow, in heaven and on earth and under the earth, and every tongue acknowledge that Jesus Christ is Lord, to the glory of God the Father" (Phil 2:9–11); "But in these last days he has spoken to us by his Son, whom he appointed heir of all things, and through whom also he made the universe. The Son is the radiance of God's glory and the exact representation of his being, sustaining all things by his powerful word. After he had provided purification for sins, he sat down at the right hand of the Majesty in heaven. So he became as much superior to the angels as the name he has inherited is superior to theirs" (Heb 1:2–4).

7

The Apostles of the Lord Jesus Christ

THE NEW TESTAMENT LETTERS, especially the writings of Paul as representative of all the apostles, provide the *evidence of how the newly established New Covenant church worshiped and served God,* which also displays a beautiful consistency with what has been said in the foregoing chapters. The New Testament is where we see the apostles, as the latter-day prophets of God, affirm plainly what the Old Testament prophets merely intimated, which is the fact of Yahweh becoming incarnate in the son given to Israel. This son was the man, Jesus of Nazareth, who was made both Lord and Messiah, the Lord of all, having been given the name above all names.

It should be honestly seen in this chapter that Paul held to the Jewish Christology that I am preaching in this book. Paul knows of only a single person God, the Father of Israel and the redeemed people of God, and the special Father of the man, Jesus, in whom God is incarnate bodily and permanently. Paul regards and speaks of the Holy Spirit as Moses did, as the mode of the special, localized presence of God (who otherwise is seated on the throne of heaven, now with the glorified Messiah beside him) indwelling, filling, and empowering the people of God.

The apostles of the Lord Jesus preached only a *gospel which was a strict fulfillment of the gospel revealed and announced by the Old Testament prophets.* These selected New Testament verses will demonstrate this important principle: "Fellow Israelites, listen to this: *Jesus of Nazareth was a man accredited by God to you* by miracles, wonders and signs, which God did among you through him, as you yourselves know" (Acts 2:22); "God has raised this Jesus to life, and we are all witnesses of it. Exalted to the right hand of God, he has received from the Father the promised Holy Spirit and has poured out what you now see and hear. For David did not ascend to heaven, and yet he said, 'The Lord said to my Lord: Sit at my right hand until I make your enemies a footstool for your feet.' Therefore let all Israel be assured of this: *God has made this Jesus, whom you crucified, both Lord and Messiah*" (Acts 2:32–36); "But this is how *God fulfilled what he had foretold through all the prophets, saying that his Messiah would suffer.* Repent, then, and turn to God, so that your sins may be wiped out, that times of refreshing may come from the Lord, and that he may send *the Messiah, who has been appointed for you—even Jesus.* Heaven must receive him until the time comes for God to restore everything, as he promised long ago through his holy prophets" (Acts 3:18–21); "Indeed, beginning with Samuel, all the prophets who have spoken have foretold these days. And you are heirs of the prophets and of the covenant God made with your fathers. He said to Abraham, 'Through your offspring all peoples on earth will be blessed.' *When God raised up his servant, he sent him first to you* to bless you by turning each of you from your wicked ways" (Acts 3:24–26); "You stiff-necked people! Your hearts and ears are still uncircumcised. You are just like your ancestors: You always resist the Holy Spirit! Was there ever a prophet your ancestors did not persecute? They even killed those *who predicted the coming of the Righteous One.* And now you have betrayed and murdered him" (Acts 7:51–52); "You know *the message God sent to the people of Israel, announcing the good news of peace through Jesus Christ, who is Lord of all*" (Acts 10:36); "We tell you the good news: *What God promised our ancestors he has fulfilled for us, their children, by raising up Jesus.* As it is written in the second Psalm: 'You are my son; today I have become your father'" (Acts 13:32–33); "But God has helped me to this very day; so I stand here and testify to small and great alike. *I am saying nothing beyond what the prophets and Moses said would happen—that the Messiah would suffer* and, as the first to rise from the dead, would bring the message of light to his own people and to the Gentiles" (Acts 26:22–23); "Paul, a servant of Christ Jesus, called to be an apostle and set apart for the gospel of God—*the gospel he promised beforehand through his prophets in the Holy Scriptures regarding his Son,* who as to his earthly life was a descendant of David, and who through the Spirit of holiness was appointed the Son of God in power by his resurrection from the dead: Jesus Christ our Lord" (Rom 1:1–4).

The apostles of the Lord Jesus were commissioned to *preach the gospel in his one name only.* Everywhere we read that in the name of Jesus was the message of salvation proclaimed. Both the apostles and the enemies of the gospel understood that the gospel was preached in the one name only:

"He told them, 'This is what is written: The Messiah will suffer and rise from the dead on the third day, and repentance for the forgiveness of sins will be preached *in his name* to all nations, beginning at Jerusalem'" (Luke 24:46–47); "Peter replied, 'Repent and be baptized, every one of you, *in the name of Jesus Christ* for the forgiveness of your sins. And you will receive the gift of the Holy Spirit'" (Acts 2:38); "Salvation is found in no one else, for there is *no other name under heaven* given to mankind by which we must be saved" (Acts 4:12). Even the enemies of the gospel, the unbelieving Jewish Sanhedrin, understood that the Christian message was being proclaimed only in the name of Jesus: " 'But to stop this thing from spreading any further among the people, we must warn them to speak no longer to anyone *in this name.*' Then they called them in again and commanded them not to speak or teach at all *in the name of Jesus*" (Acts 4:17–18).

It is extremely important to realize that in the narrative account of the spreading church in the book of Acts, the unbelieving Jews never raise the charge of blasphemy regarding the dogma of the Trinity, nor do they even dispute the Trinity dogma as one of the reasons for their opposition to the Christian message. Rabbinic Judaism, to this day, would repudiate the dogma of the Trinity as blasphemous and foreign to the revelation of Moses. But in the narrative account of the book of Acts, there is absolutely no irritation about the Trinity dogma at all. The apostles do not bother to mention it as necessary to know for salvation. The unbelieving Jews are nowhere offended about it. It is as a non-existent matter. This can only be explained by the fact that *the Trinity dogma was never preached or taught by the apostles of the Lord Jesus to the nascent church at all,* as there is no mention of the Trinity dogma in the accounts of the apostolic sermons, and no offense taken of the Christian message by the unbelieving Jews on its account.

The famous baptismal formula found in Matthew 28:19 ("in the name of the Father and of the Son and of the Holy Spirit") is suspicious and completely foreign and antithetical to the rest of the Bible. It is probably a scribal insertion similar to the factual insertion of a trinitarian statement in 1 John 5:7 found in the older King James Version Bible. The formula is ambiguous and proves heretical modalism just as well as "orthodox" trinitarianism. The formula verse is the only mention of a supposed Trinity in the entire Bible and is inconsistent with the rest of scripture. It is found in the middle of a series of statements by Jesus where he speaks about himself with singular pronouns. In the same Gospel of Matthew, Jesus shows no knowledge of a Trinity. The flow of the "great commission" passage would be better with Jesus commanding baptism in *his name alone* as Luke-Acts reports (Luke 24:47; Acts 2:38; Acts 8:16; Acts 10:48; etc. And see John 20:31). The trinitarian explanation asserting that the name of the three members of the supposed Trinity are represented in the one name of Jesus Christ is silly and unconvincing.

The New Testament writing apostles provided statements of belief, or creeds, in their letters, which are extremely important to consider for my argument. The theological creeds of the New Testament might be unnecessary as the Jews, for many centuries, have had their creed of Moses firmly entrenched within biblical Judaism. But the New Testament creeds are now necessary because of the fact of the incarnation of God in the man Jesus, which gives rise to an addendum, as it were. The writing apostles of the New Testament provided several incarnational creeds. These theological creeds utilize the Jewish *Shema* creed found in Deuteronomy 6, which is foundational to Mosaic Judaism. The Israelites were provided this one creed by Moses, and all that was necessary for the Israelites to understand was that there was only one true God who made the entire universe by himself, and his name is Yahweh. Moses expands on the singular person of Yahweh as being the Father of Israel. The *Shema* states simply that there is only Yahweh as the only God in the universe to fear and love.

But for the New Testament church, there needed to be provided a creed that contains the important and amazing *addition of the person of the Messiah, Jesus, in whom God is now permanently incarnated bodily.* Paul provided several creeds which contain this amazing addition. The creed written to the Corinthian church utilizes the Jewish *Shema* creed. But Paul adapts it to state twice the reality of the two persons who share the divine throne of heaven now: "Yet for us there is but one God, the Father, from whom all things came and for whom we live; and there is but one Lord, Jesus Christ, through whom all things came and through whom we live" (1 Cor 8:6). Paul first states the well-known Jewish creed that there is only one true God, known as the Father of Israel, who also made all things directly by his supernatural power. This Creator-glory is the unique glory of the living God. Paul then repeats the statement saying that there is only one true Lord, who is the man Jesus Christ. Then Paul credits the unique glory of the Creator to Jesus because of the incarnation. Paul is not saying that Jesus is a mere agent of creation, as the fictional Trinity dogma asserts, but that through Jesus' being the incarnate God, all things came into being through him and exist for him. The mere agent idea is also refuted because *the all things were created for him,* the man Jesus, for the divine terminus within him. Paul will more clearly state this fact in the creed found in the letter to the Colossian church.

The creed written to the Philippian church, possibly utilizing a preexistent creedal song of the early church, states the important truths that Jesus Christ was in the role of God but who chose, in humility, to "empty" or *suppress his role as God* in order to live the role of an ordinary man in order to fulfill his mission of grace for the redemption of God's people: "In your relationships with one another, have the same mindset as Christ Jesus: Who, being in very nature God, did not consider equality with God something to be used to his own advantage; rather, he made himself nothing by taking the very nature of a servant, being made in human likeness. And being found in appearance as a man, he humbled himself by becoming obedient to death—even death on a cross!" (Phil 2:5–8).

It is extremely important to realize that whenever Paul is speaking about the Lord Jesus Christ, he is thinking first of the man, in whom God is incarnate. Paul does not have in mind the Trinity fiction of an "eternal Son" who then became incarnate in the man, Jesus. The trinitarians inevitably misread this Philippian passage as saying that the supposed "divine Son" was the one who was in the "form" of God, and then who emptied himself, which is nonsense and confusion.

Also, because of the influence of the Trinity dogma, the term Paul uses, "form," is interpreted as "the very nature," implying a divine-metaphysical-essence nuance. But this cannot be correct because Paul will use it easily with the statement about the servant's existence in verse 7. The term must serve either statement easily. I believe the best English sense is the idea of a "role." Supporting this interpretation is the term that the NIV Bible translates as "being": "being in very nature as God" (v 6). The term is *huparchon*. This term is not the word that denotes simple 'being,' which is *ontos*. Rather, this term is commonly used closer to its true definition, which is "possession" of a quality or status. Paul is saying that the man Jesus *possessed the role* of being equal to God due to the incarnation of God in him bodily—"being" in the role of God.

Then Paul says a very meaningful statement, in my paraphrasing, "Have this humbling attitude in yourselves as was in Jesus Christ (the man in whom God is incarnate, and which renders the man Jesus to be equal to God in heaven) who, possessing the role of God, did not think it robbery, or inappropriate, to be equal to God (in heaven), nevertheless he emptied himself (*alla heauton ekenosen*) of this equality-role as God and, instead, took the role of an ordinary man for the sake of obedience for redemption."

We must be careful to notice that *it is not God who is emptying himself* of the role of God. Rather, it is the man, Jesus, who was existing in the role of God, being the very incarnation of God; he suppressed this role of equality with God and lived and behaved as an ordinary man serving his God. The additional phrase in verse 8 helps us to understand this: "And being found in appearance as a man, *he humbled himself*, etc." Jesus humbled himself. That is why Paul exhorts the Philippian church to have the same attitude of humility, regarding other believers as more important for the sake of loving service.

We must also notice that Paul here never uses the term "the Son," or "the Son of God." He does not teach the fiction that an "eternal Son of God," the second member of a supposed Trinity, became the incarnate one. Paul always regards Jesus Christ, the Jewish flesh and blood man, as the "Son of God." Paul, and all the New Testament writers, always describe Jesus as behaving, and having qualities, and having susceptibilities, as a real human being, and which statements *cannot be applied to a supposed "eternal Son of God,"* as these selected verses will demonstrate: "But the gift is not like the trespass. For if the many died by the trespass of the one man, how much more did God's grace and the gift that came by the grace of *the one man, Jesus Christ,* overflow to the many!" (Rom 5:15); "By his power God *raised the Lord from the dead,* and he will raise us also" (1 Cor 6:14); "But Christ has indeed been raised from the dead, the firstfruits of those who have fallen asleep. For since death came through a man, *the resurrection of the dead comes also through a man.* For as in Adam all die, so in Christ all will be made alive" (1 Cor 15:20–22); "I have been *crucified with Christ* and I no longer live, but Christ lives in me. The life I now live in the body, I live by faith in the Son of God, who loved me and *gave himself for me"* (Gal 2:20); "But when the set time had fully come, God sent his Son, *born of a woman, born under the law"* (Gal 4:4); "For there is one God and one mediator between God and mankind, *the man Christ Jesus"* (1 Tim 2:5); "Remember Jesus Christ, *raised from the dead, descended from David.* This is my gospel" (2 Tim 2:8); "But in these last days he has spoken to us by his Son, whom he *appointed heir of all things,* and through whom also he made the universe. The Son is the radiance of God's glory and the exact representation of his being, sustaining all things by his powerful word. After he had *provided purification for sins,* he sat down at the right hand of the Majesty in heaven. So he became as much superior to the angels as the name he has inherited is superior to theirs" (Heb 1:2–4); "But if we walk in the light, as he is in the light, we have fellowship with one another, and *the blood of Jesus, his Son,* purifies us from all sin" (1 John 1:7).

The creed written to the Colossian church, found mainly in Colossians 1:15–20 (but is also succinctly stated in Colossians 2:9), is a long theological statement describing the glory of the Son of God, consisting of his Lordship over all the universe, and his headship over the church. This creed specifically asserts what is the divine basis as to how he is glorious: *Jesus is glorious by virtue of the incarnation of God in him bodily.* However, as usual, the trinitarians like to read into any passage that addresses the Son of God, who is the anointed servant Jesus, qualities belonging to the fictional "eternal Son of God," but which inevitably causes confusion to a thinking person. But the reality is that Paul is here addressing *the man Jesus,* who is the Son of God's love, as he just mentioned in the previous verses 12–14. Paul is describing the very man who shed his blood on the cross for the believer's "redemption, the forgiveness of sins."

Very simply, in this passage, Paul declares why Jesus is the glorious Lord of the entire universe, and then why he is the head of the church. Regarding the first item, Paul declares, "The Son is the image of the invisible God, the firstborn over all creation. For in him all things were created: things in heaven and on earth, visible and invisible, whether thrones or powers or rulers or authorities; all things have been created through him and for him. He is before all things, and in him all things hold together" (vv 15–17). And regarding the second item, Paul declares, "And he is the head of the body, the church; he is the beginning and the firstborn from among the dead, so that in everything he might have the supremacy" (v 18). Then Paul explains how Jesus can have this supremacy: "For God was pleased to have all his fulness dwell in him" (v 19), and this declaration is more fully expressed in Colossians 2:9, with unmistakable terms: "For in Christ all the fulness of the Deity lives in bodily form." This causal declaration begins with a certain Greek phrase: *hoti en auto*, "because in him." That is, because God is in him, therefore, etc. This Greek phrase is used three times in relation to the incarnation: Colossians 1:16, 19, and 2:9.

Some notices must be mentioned since the English Bible versions can be somewhat misleading, and there usually is a trinitarian bias to the translations. It is extremely important to see that in verse 16, Paul says all things were not only "created through him," *but also "for him" (kai eis auton)*. This last clause *only indicates the glory of God himself* before the fact of the incarnation. Paul always changes the creation preposition that is only used for God himself, "by" to "through" for the Messiah. Paul knows that Jesus is first considered a man who cannot create anything by himself. But *through the incarnation* Jesus can be *given the credit for the creation of the world since the Creator himself lives bodily in him*. Paul honors Jesus equally and in the same causal and purposive sense as God the Creator, as he says elsewhere, "For from him and through him and for him *(kai eis auton)* are all things. To him be the glory forever! Amen" (Rom 11:36). Therefore, Paul knows of no creation agency of the fictional "eternal Son." All things were made for the Messiah. Then Paul declares that because God was pleased to have all his fulness of Deity live in Jesus bodily, the Messiah can be worshiped as God himself.

Paul further says in the Colossian creed regarding the Messiah's divine glory that "He is before all things, and in him all things hold together" (v 17). This, again, is Paul's inspired crediting of the divine glory of God to the Messiah. This verse is usually misread by the trinitarians to say that

Jesus "existed before all things." But the Greek language provides a better reading: *kai autos estin pro panton kai ta panta en auto sunestaken.* Paul says more literally, He "is" (*estin*) before all things. That is, presently, he is *in the first place of importance before all things, even as God is.* If Paul had actually meant to say that Jesus, the man, had existed before all things (which thing is a blasphemous impossibility), would he not have used the past tense verb "was" since the fact of having existed before all things would now be in the past? Even when John records the praise of the Lord God in Revelation 1:8 and 4:8, God's eternal pre-existence relative to the universe is described as he "who was" (*ho an*). But more logically, Paul is saying that Jesus is before all things in the sense of importance, presently, due to the incarnation.

Paul also says that *all things are held together;* elsewhere explained, *by his powerful word* (see Heb 1:3), which is precisely the glory of God the Father himself rather than a supposed agent of creation, as these verses prove: "Let all the earth fear the LORD (Yahweh, the Father); let all the people of the world revere him. *For he spoke,* and it came to be; *he commanded,* and it stood firm" (Ps 33:8–9); "By faith we understand that the universe was formed *at God's command,* so that what is seen was not made out of what was visible" (Heb 11:3); "But they deliberately forget that long ago *by God's word* the heavens came into being and the earth was formed out of water and by water. By these waters also the world of that time was deluged and destroyed. *By the same word* the present heavens and earth are reserved for fire, being kept for the day of judgment and destruction of the ungodly" (2 Pet 3:5–7).

The letter written to the Hebrews, chapter 1, verses 1–14, if read carefully and honestly and without trinitarian bias, provides the church with almost a demonstration as to how the unique divine glory of the one true God is credited or ascribed to the Messiah, Jesus. When the trinitarians misread the first chapter of the letter to the Hebrews, they read about an "eternal son of God" because they employ the circular reasoning which is inevitable from first misreading the prologue to the Gospel of John. But when we read the letter with the correct antecedent theology of Moses and the Hebrew prophets, we know that God finally speaking by "his Son" means a man dearly loved and commissioned rather than a supernatural being existing from the eternal past. We also will read that this Son was "appointed heir of all things" (v 2), with the meaningful sense that before his work of redemption, he *did not inherently own all things* but was *granted this honor* because no ordinary man could ever be owner and Lord of the "ages," as the Greek word literally reads.

Again, this "Son" was susceptible to offering his body as a guilt offering, slain to provide "purification for sins," and only then "sat down at the right hand of the Majesty of heaven" (v 3), who would also begin his intercessory role as the church's great high priest, appointed by God and not by himself, as the writer to the Hebrews teaches: "Therefore, since we have a great high priest who has ascended into heaven, Jesus the Son of God, let us hold firmly to the faith we profess" (Heb 4:14); and "Such a high priest truly meets our need—one who is *holy, blameless, pure, set apart from sinners,* exalted above the heavens. Unlike the other high priests, he does not need to offer sacrifices day after day, first for his own sins, and then for the sins of the people. He sacrificed for their sins once for all when *he offered himself.* For the law appoints as high priests men in all their weakness; but the oath, which came after the law, appointed the Son, who has been *made perfect forever*" (Heb 7:26–28). Such significant sacerdotal accomplishments cannot be said of a fictional "eternal Son."

Jesus is not the "eternally existent Son" as the trinitarians always insist because then the significant *comparisons* between the Son and the angels of God, which the writer to the Hebrews makes, would all be tautological and senseless. He is not comparing an eternal divine being with the angels! He is not comparing God with his angels! The supposed "God the Son" would not need to be appointed an heir of all things, nor be invited to share the divine throne, because he would already own all things and would already be the God of the universe.

Rather, the writer is teaching how much more blessed by God is the man Jesus than any of the angels ever were in this matter of *being invited and appointed to share the divine glory of God,* as he says, "So he became as much superior to the angels *as the name he has inherited* is superior to theirs. For to which of the angels did God ever say, 'You are my Son; today I have become your Father'? Or again, 'I will be his Father, and he will be my Son'? And again, when God brings his firstborn into the world, he says, 'Let all God's angels worship him'" (Heb 1:4–6); "To which of the angels did God ever say, 'Sit at my right hand until I make your enemies a footstool for your feet'" (Heb 1:13).

The writer of the letter to the Hebrews provides, as it were, an illustration of how the glory of Yahweh, the Creator and Redeemer of Israel, is *ascribed to the man Jesus by virtue of the incarnation of God in him bodily.* It is important to understand that these ascriptions of divine glory to the firstborn son of God *are not being said by Yahweh alone.* For then it would seem to be true that there are other members of the Godhead, and so trinitarianism would seem to be a truth. But rather, *these ascriptions are being said through the inspired prophets*—just as we correctly read Psalm 102 originally.

The incarnation was evidently from the birth of the Messiah, who is the son given to Israel: "And again, when God brings his firstborn into the world, he says, 'Let all God's angels worship him'" (Heb 1:6). Then the glory of the divine throne is ascribed to this son brought into the world: "But about the Son he says, 'Your throne, O God, will last for ever and ever; a scepter of justice will be the scepter of your kingdom'" (Heb 1:8). We know that the glory of the divine throne and kingdom is being ascribed to a man now because of the further praise of the character of this man, and the mention of his companions that are found, and his being anointed with oil, which things can only be said of a man: "You have loved righteousness and hated wickedness; therefore God, your God, has set you above your companions by anointing you with the oil of joy" (Heb 1:9).

Then the unique Creator-glory of Yahweh is ascribed to this son brought into the world: "He also says, 'In the beginning, Lord, you laid the foundations of the earth, and the heavens are the work of your hands. They will perish, but you remain; they will all wear out like a garment. You will roll them up like a robe; like a garment they will be changed. But you remain the same, and your years will never end'" (Heb 1:10–12).

Then the writer to the Hebrews reminds them that all of these ascriptions of divine glory to the son brought into the world have their original cause by the amazing invitation for this son of David to sit at the right hand of God: "To which of the angels did God ever say, 'Sit at my right hand until I make your enemies a footstool for your feet'" (Heb 1:13).

If we have correctly understood how the writer to the Hebrews considers the man Jesus to be worshiped as God, then we can easily see that all the apostles hold the same conviction and express it succinctly in their writings. This is how John recognizes the incarnation of God in the man Jesus in his famous prologue statement, after first stating that when Jesus started the gospel ministry, he was completely devoted to God, and also that "Through him all things were made; without him nothing was made that has been made" (John 1:3); and again, "He was in the world, *and though the world was made through him,* the world did not recognize him" (John 1:10). This is the clear understanding of the hosts of heaven in their worship of God Almighty: "You are worthy, our Lord and God, to receive glory and honor and power, *for you created all things,* and by your will they were created and have their being" (Rev 4:11).

The writer to the Hebrews shows us not the fiction of the agency of the supposed "second member of the Godhead," but rather a direct crediting of the full glory of God to the man Jesus when he is brought into the world. Elsewhere in his letter, he credits all of the work of creation to the lone work of God himself: "In bringing many sons and daughters to glory, it was fitting that God, *for whom and through whom everything exists,* should make the pioneer of their salvation perfect through what he suffered" (Heb 2:10). Paul does the same in his preaching to the Gentiles: "The God who made the world and everything in it is the Lord of heaven and earth and does not live in temples built by human hands. And he is not served by human hands, as if he needed anything. Rather, *he himself gives everyone life and breath and everything else*" (Acts 17:24–25).

Paul often used triads in his writings. He seems to be fond of heaping up terms for emphasis. Some of these triadic statements are inevitably used by the trinitarians as proof-texts. The most famous trinitarian go-to triadic statement text is 2 Corinthians 13:14, where Paul requests, "May the grace of the Lord Jesus Christ, and the love of God, and the fellowship of the Holy Spirit be with you all." This verse is seen as an evident regard for the Trinity by the apostle Paul. But it is not. I believe the most critical principle to bear in mind whenever we read any New Testament verse that mentions the Holy Spirit is to read *with the understanding that the Old Testament Jews had regarding the Spirit: that it was well-known as the special presence of Yahweh—*not a third person to be worshiped as the Catholic Nicene creed asserts. We have no right to disregard the antecedent theology of the Old Testament. So, when Jesus the Jewish Messiah talks about another Advocate in the sending of the Holy Spirit, we must keep in mind that he is speaking as a Jewish man whose theology was influenced by Old Testament categories—not post-New Testament Catholic categories. And when the Jewish apostle Paul mentions the Holy Spirit interceding for us, he first regards the Spirit as the localized, indwelling, special presence of God in the believer—not a third person to be worshiped, as the post-New Testament Catholic creed asserts.

Therefore, this verse in 2 Corinthians 13:14 is a concluding prayer request for the Corinthian believers. It is not an acknowledgement of the supposed Trinity. Three particular blessings are asked by Paul, all of which are to be subjectively experienced by the believers in their own hearts and lives: (1) Paul asks that the grace of the Lord Jesus Christ be "with" them. He is not asking that they would know about the general grace of the Lord Jesus in the gospel message—they already knew this. He is asking that the supernatural grace of strength and encouragement would be with them experientially—that they would be powerfully helped and changed by it. (2) He is asking that the love of God be "with" the believers. They already knew about the love of God in the gospel message. He is asking that the love of God would be felt and experienced more deeply by them in their walk. (3) He is asking that the supernatural influence of the special presence of God would be increasingly theirs, and by which the other blessings are felt and experienced.

This is not a worship text for the supposed Trinity. This is not praise offered, but requests pleaded for the believers. The order of the triad in this verse is incorrect according to the Trinity dogma: Lord Jesus

Christ-God-Holy Spirit. When Paul does praise God at the beginning of the letter to the Corinthians, he mentions only God the Father and the Lord Jesus Christ—the Spirit of God is omitted (2 Cor 1:3). The Spirit of God is omitted because Paul is a Jew who knows his Old Testament, and he knows that the Holy Spirit is the special presence of God—not a separate third person to be worshiped.

One extremely important triadic statement written by Paul is rather conveniently overlooked by the trinitarians: "I charge you, *in the sight of God and Christ Jesus and the elect angels,* to keep these instructions without partiality, and to do nothing out of favoritism" (1 Tim 5:21). This verse is similar to two other statements, which are not triadic but which demonstrate the truth that, for Paul, there are only two persons who share the divine throne to appeal to for divine authority and exhortation: "In the sight of God, who gives life to everything, and of Christ Jesus, who while testifying before Pontius Pilate made the good confession, I charge you to keep this command without spot or blame until the appearing of our Lord Jesus Christ" (1 Tim 6:13–14); and here, Paul says succinctly that God alone *gives life to everything*—no divine agency is recognized. And also, "In the presence of God and of Christ Jesus, who will judge the living and the dead, and in view of his appearing and his kingdom, I give you this charge" (2 Tim 4:1).

Another Trinity proof-text is found in Romans 8:26–27: "In the same way, the Spirit helps us in our weakness. We do not know what we ought to pray for, but the Spirit himself intercedes for us through wordless groans. And he who searches our hearts knows the mind of the Spirit, because the Spirit intercedes for God's people in accordance with the will of God." Again, I believe the most critical principle to bear in mind whenever we read any New Testament verse that mentions the Holy Spirit is to read *with the understanding that the Old Testament Jews had regarding the Spirit: that it was well-known as the special presence of Yahweh*—not a third person to be worshiped as the Catholic Nicene creed asserts. And again, we have no right to disregard the antecedent theology of the Old Testament. So, again, when Jesus talks about another Advocate in the sending of the Holy Spirit, we must keep in mind that he is speaking as a Jewish man whose theology was influenced by Old Testament categories—not post-New Testament Catholic categories. And, again, when the Jewish apostle Paul mentions the Holy Spirit interceding for us, he first regards the Spirit as the localized, indwelling, special presence of God in the believer—not a third person to be worshiped, as the post-New Testament Catholic creed asserts.

When Paul says the Spirit "intercedes for us," Paul is not saying the Spirit is doing the actual praying to God. (This then looks as though there really are two distinct persons in mind here!) Rather, the Spirit (in the mode of the special presence of God) is helping believers by inducing the wordless prayers in their hearts, which they do not know they should pray when they do not know what to pray at times! God is not praying to himself. Paul is comforting the Christian believers that his presence helps us to pray wisely when we do not know what to pray because it is according to the will of God, and he knows what is being prayed because he searches the hearts and so knows what these wordless groans are.

Therefore, Paul is merely saying that God in heaven *knows what his indwelling presence in the heart of the believer is inducing because God in heaven is the searcher of the hearts to begin with.* In other words, God's Spirit is not doing the actual groaning, but the believer is, because *the presence of God is inducing these wordless groans in the heart of the believer.* The wordless groans are the believer's feelings. And then God perceives the secret emotions of the heart which were induced by the help of his indwelling presence. God himself helps believers to pray to him when they do not know what to pray. Nowhere in scripture does God and the Spirit communicate with each other as distinct personages. Jesus never prays to, or worships, the Spirit alongside the Father. We should worship God as Jesus, the perfect Israelite, worshiped his God—not as the Catholics think we should.

An extremely important evidence demonstrating *the theological convictions of the apostles regarding how they worshiped and served God* is to be found in their inspired letters written to the churches. The greetings and conclusions of their letters indicate their understanding and their reverence of God and his kingdom. The apostle Paul, as representative of the apostolic Christianity of the early church, obviously held to the Mosaic understanding of the Godhead, and therefore wrote his letter greetings in a manner which proves a beautiful consistency with the antecedent theology of Moses and the Hebrew prophets. Look wherever you will, all the greetings and doxologies of his letters mention reverent worship, and praise, and acknowledgement, and prayers toward the two persons who now share the divine throne, as these selected verses will show: "To all in Rome who are loved by God and called to be his holy people: Grace and peace to you *from God our Father and from the Lord Jesus Christ*" (Rom 1:7); "Grace and peace to you *from God our Father and the Lord Jesus Christ*" (1 Cor 1:3); "Grace and peace to you *from God our Father and the Lord Jesus Christ*" (2 Cor 1:2); "Grace and peace to you *from God our Father and the Lord Jesus Christ*" (Gal 1:3); "Grace and peace to you *from God our Father and the Lord Jesus Christ*" (Eph 1:2); "*To him (the Father) be glory in the church and in Christ Jesus* throughout all generations, for ever and ever! Amen" (Eph 3:21); "For of this you can be sure: No immoral, impure or greedy person—such a person is an idolater—has any inheritance in *the kingdom of Christ and of God*"

(Eph 5:5); "Peace to the brothers and sisters, and love with faith *from God the Father and the Lord Jesus Christ"* (Eph 6:23); "Paul, Silas and Timothy, To the church of the Thessalonians *in God the Father and the Lord Jesus Christ:* Grace and peace to you" (1 Thess 1:1); "Now may *our God and Father himself and our Lord Jesus* clear the way for us to come to you" (1 Thess 3:11); "May he strengthen your hearts so that you will be blameless and holy *in the presence of our God and Father when our Lord Jesus comes* with all his holy ones" (1 Thess 3:13); "May the Lord direct your hearts *into God's love and Christ's perseverance"* (2 Thess 3:5).

The other writing apostles worshiped with the same theological convictions, as these few verses show: "James, *a servant of God and of the Lord Jesus Christ,* To the twelve tribes scattered among the nations: Greetings" (James 1:1). *"Praise be to the God and Father of our Lord Jesus Christ!* In his great mercy he has given us new birth into a living hope through the resurrection of Jesus Christ from the dead" (1 Pet 1:3); and here, though Peter recognizes, in the previous verse, the work of the Spirit in the believers' sanctification, still he offers no praise directly to the Spirit as a separate personage. "Grace and peace be yours in abundance *through the knowledge of God and of Jesus our Lord"* (2 Pet 1:2); and here, Peter prays for the enjoyment of grace and peace, which are to be had through the knowledge of the two persons who share the divine throne. He specifically *delimits the knowledge toward the two persons* of God the Father and the Lord Jesus Christ. The Holy Spirit is shamefully omitted. "Grace, mercy and peace *from God the Father and from Jesus Christ, the Father's Son,* will be with us in truth and love" (2 John 3). And lastly, Jude's greeting: "Jude, a servant of Jesus Christ and a brother of James, To those who have been called, who are loved *in God the Father and kept for Jesus Christ:* Mercy, peace and love be yours in abundance" (Jude 1–2).

When a scriptural writer of the ancient world wanted to speak of the *presence* of someone, the writer would use a term that refers more literally to the face; and by metaphorical extension, one's presence would be referred to. This would be the usage whether the writer was referring to either God, who is pure immaterial Spirit, or to men. The writers of the New Testament scriptures happen to speak of either the "face" or the presence of both God the Father and the Lord Jesus Christ. The face of God would be anthropomorphically understood, while the face of the glorious Lord Jesus Christ may be literally understood but having spiritual significance. But the Holy Spirit is never mentioned as having a "face" because the Spirit of God is not regarded as a distinct personage to be worshiped but is the special presence of God. We read of the face of either God the Father or the exalted Lord Jesus Christ: "See that you do not despise one of these little ones. For I tell you that their angels in heaven always see *the face of my Father in heaven*" (Matt 18:10). Notice, again, that the face of God is only the face of the Father of the Messiah. No Trinity is honored by Jesus. And also, "For God, who said, 'Let light shine out of darkness,' made his light shine in our hearts to give us the light of the knowledge of God's glory displayed in *the face of Christ*" (2 Cor 4:6).

Again, the book of the Revelation written by the apostle John, depicting the unhindered perspective of heavenly worship, evidences an indisputable delimitation of two persons, each with majestic names, sharing the one divine throne by the testimony of John and the testimony of the Lamb of God himself: "The one who is victorious I will make a pillar in the temple of my God. Never again will they leave it. I will write on them *the name of my God* and the name of the city of my God, the new Jerusalem, which is coming down out of heaven from my God; and I will also write on them *my new name*" (Rev 3:12); "Then I looked, and there before me was the Lamb, standing on Mount Zion, and with him 144,000 who had *his name and his Father's name* written on their foreheads" (Rev 14:1). The apostles affirm the reality of only two persons enthroned in heaven, each having a majestic name, a glorious face, and a terrifying presence, formed by the union of the two natures of divinity and humanity, which provides a beautiful consistency with the arithmetical anticipation of the Hebrew prophets.

The expressions of the apostle Paul actually refute the dogma of the Trinity, if read honestly by the trinitarians. Not everything that the apostle says about Christ is seriously weighed in the trinitarians' selective theologizing. Paul regards the Lord Jesus Christ not as the supposed second member, being co-equal and co-eternal in divine majesty with God the Father but rather as the man in whom Yahweh is incarnate. But the Messiah is also subordinate to the Father, and Jesus will relinquish the kingdom back to God, that God may be all in all, as these verses show: "But I want you to realize that the head of every man is Christ, and the head of the woman is man, and *the head of Christ is God*" (1 Cor 11:3); "Then the end will come, when [Christ] *hands over the kingdom to God the Father* after he has destroyed all dominion, authority, and power. For he must reign until he has put all his enemies under his feet. The last enemy to be destroyed is death. For he 'has put everything under his feet.' Now when it says that 'everything' has been put under him, it is clear that *this does not include God himself, who put everything under Christ.* When he has done this, *then the Son himself will be made subject to him who put everything under him, so that God may be all in all*" (1 Cor 15:24–28); "For you died, and your life is *now hidden with Christ in God*" (Col 3:3).

It is worth mentioning the New Testament fact of how the writing apostles regarded Yahweh of the Old Testament revelation as being now incarnate in the man Jesus Christ in such simple terms that they were comfortable with substituting the term "Jesus" or "Christ" in certain places where the passages originally or naturally refer to Yahweh, as seen in these selected passages, which sense eliminates the nonsensical "Christophany" interpretations: "Isaiah said this because he saw Jesus' glory and spoke about him" (John 12:41); "You, however, are not in the realm of the flesh but are in the realm of the Spirit, if indeed the Spirit of God lives in you. And if anyone does not have the Spirit of Christ, they do not belong to Christ" (Rom 8:9); "They all ate the same spiritual food and drank the same spiritual drink; for they drank from the spiritual rock that accompanied them, and that rock was Christ" (1 Cor 10:3–4); "We should not test Christ, as some of them did—and were killed by snakes" (1 Cor 10:9); "For I know that through your prayers and God's provision of the Spirit of Jesus Christ what has happened to me will turn out for my deliverance" (Phil 1:19); "He regarded disgrace for the sake of Christ as of greater value than the treasures of Egypt, because he was looking ahead to his reward" (Heb 11:26).

When a Jewish person especially came to saving faith in the prophesied Messiah, the writer of the letter to the Hebrews describes this spiritual change as coming to the joyful mountain of spiritual Zion rather than the mountain of fear, which was the experience of the Hebrews entering into the Mosaic covenant: "But you have come to Mount Zion, to the city of the living God, the heavenly Jerusalem. You have come to thousands upon thousands of angels in joyful assembly, to the church of the firstborn, whose names are written in heaven. You have come to God, the Judge of all, to the spirits of the righteous made perfect, to Jesus the mediator of a new covenant, and to the sprinkled blood that speaks a better word than the blood of Abel" (Heb 12:22–24). The writer lists what is encountered: he mentions God the Judge of all, which is how Yahweh the Father of Israel would have been known to the Jews; he mentions Jesus the mediator who sprinkled his blood; and he mentions both the angels and the redeemed persons. But he does not mention the Holy Spirit because the Jews understood the Spirit of God to be the special presence of God.

The apostle Paul bothers to reiterate the core, unnegotiable gospel message, but he nowhere spends a breath asserting the supposed momentous and unnegotiable dogma that insists the Godhead is composed of three eternal persons in one essence! Paul says, "For what I have received I passed on to you *as of first importance*: that Christ died for our sins according to the Scriptures, that he was buried, that he was raised on the third day according to the Scriptures" (1 Cor 15:3–4). The rest of his words listing the appearance of Jesus to certain individuals or groups are not necessarily a part of the core gospel message, and so Paul does not say, "according to the Scriptures," regarding these appearances. However, what is indisputable is that he honors no Trinity nor insists that this fiction is a real and necessary component of the gospel message for one to be saved. Also, Paul had already asserted the theological creed which is also arguably necessary for the core gospel message in 1 Corinthians 8:6 saying that there is only one true God, who is the Father and Creator, and also there is one Lord Jesus Christ, for the church of believers. And nowhere does any one of the apostles show the acumen to invent the terminology of "God the Son" and "God the Spirit" to be breathed out with "God the Father" as our perceptive trinitarian theologians have!

The apostle Paul succinctly describes the church with these following few words, which actually demonstrate the Jewish Christology that my book preaches: "For it is we who are the circumcision, we who *serve God by his Spirit,* who boast in Christ Jesus, and who put no confidence in the flesh" (Phil 3:3). Paul says believers serve, or worship, God *by* his Spirit—they do not worship the Spirit itself as distinct from God. Such a practice is the lie of the Catholic Nicene creed.